*Psychology and Religion
for Everyday Living*

THE MACMILLAN COMPANY
NEW YORK · BOSTON · CHICAGO
DALLAS · ATLANTA · SAN FRANCISCO

MACMILLAN AND CO., LIMITED
LONDON · BOMBAY · CALCUTTA
MADRAS · MELBOURNE

**THE MACMILLAN COMPANY
OF CANADA, LIMITED**
TORONTO

CHARLES T. HOLMAN

PSYCHOLOGY
and
RELIGION
for
EVERYDAY LIVING

NEW YORK : *The Macmillan Company* : 1951

In Loving and Grateful Memory
of my son

CHARLES MONTGOMERY HOLMAN

R.C.A.F., U.S.A.A.F.

Killed in Line of Duty
at Ditchingham, England,
July 6th, 1944.

 Greater love hath no man than this,
that a man lay down his life
for his friends. JOHN 15:13.

PREFACE

MEN EVERYWHERE and always have sought a satisfying life. But hindrances, frustrations, anxieties, disappointments, and defeats are, in varying measure, the lot of all men. Two thousand years ago there appeared One who said that He came that men "might have life, and have it more abundantly." How may that abundant life be achieved? How may men overcome their frustrations and defeats? How may life be brought to its true fulfilment?

This book is intended to indicate how an understanding of ourselves and of the resources inherent in religious faith may assist us in achieving a full, rich and liberated life. It does not present a systematized treatment of psychology or of religion, but it does discuss some of the problems which we all face day by day as we pursue the quest for life, and inquires what help psychology and religion can give us toward finding solutions for these problems and toward realizing life at its best.

The psychological point of view taken is that of dynamic psychology. It sees the driving forces of human life as closely related to organic processes, and the mind as an instrument of adjustment to the Reality with which the individual must come to terms. Organic hungers clamor for gratification, impulses drive relentlessly forward, the "ego" seeks its satisfactions, but when some blocking occurs a way

vii

must be found to adjust these needs and drives to the possibilities which the environment affords. The making of this adjustment is the function of the "psyche." Sometimes an adjustment is made in devious and subtle ways; sometimes the capacities for abstract thought, careful analysis, reasoning and constructive imagination are brought into play, and an intelligent adjustment is made. This is, of course, the type of adjustment which enlists the highest capacities of man, and is the one most to be desired. But men are not always reasonable. Most adjustments are probably made on a more primitive level, and often the mind is called in later to give a rational explanation of behavior dictated by impulse or passion rather than reason. This is what the psychologist calls "rationalization." It is important, if we are to understand ourselves, to recognize how the mind works in order that we may increasingly bring our conduct under the control of reason and conscience. "Know thyself!" was the wise dictum of the ancient Greeks.

The book, moreover, is written frankly from the point of view of religious faith. It maintains that the Reality to which adjustment must be made is not simply a physical universe and a human culture, but a Will and Purpose operating through all the processes of the physical and social environment in which our lives are set. As science probes more deeply into and achieves a better understanding of the processes of the physical world the mind of God is better understood. In the same way, as we humans live together and explore, experiment with, and test social rela-

*inviolable = not to be profaned, or broken
to be kept as a sanctuary*

tionships, we come increasingly to understand the will of God for human society. The sanctions by which we live, and the structures of value by which we judge the worth of our actions, are not our human inventions but belong to the eternal nature of things.

As Plato says in *The Laws,* God, not man, is the measure of all things. "Justice always follows them and punishes those who fall short of the Divine law. To the law, he who would be happy holds fast and follows it in all humility and order; but he who is lifted up with pride . . . and thinks that he has no need of a guide or ruler . . . is utterly deserted of God. . . . In a short time he pays the penalty of justice and is utterly destroyed, and his family and state with him."

This moral order—the "justice" and "Divine law" of which Plato speaks—is the will of God. It is as inviolable as the law of gravitation. It is to this order, as truly as to the order of the physical universe, that adjustment must be made if abundant life is to be achieved.

But religion not only recognizes this moral order as the will of God, and calls upon men to harmonize their wayward wills and purposes with it; it also invites men to a fellowship with God which both enriches life and enables them to do His will. Furthermore, it reveals a redeeming element at work, forgiving our failures, aiding our strivings, and welcoming men to share the friendship of God. "For thus saith the high and lofty One that inhabiteth eternity, whose name is Holy; I dwell in the high and holy place with him also that is of a contrite and humble spirit."

The author wishes to thank the authors and publishers who have so generously permitted quotations, and asks that if any quotations have been made for which he has inadvertently failed to secure proper permission, he may be pardoned.

CHARLES T. HOLMAN.

CONTENTS

Psychology and Religion
for Everyday Living

CHAPTER I

"Train Up a Child . . ."

IN AN ARMY camp on the Pacific Coast during the last war I met a young soldier who had become a problem to himself, to the other soldiers in his outfit, and to his commanding officer. He was physically strong, much above average in intelligence, and personally likable. But he was worried sick, unable to attend to his duties, and was wrecking the efficiency of the unit of which he was a member. His inadequacy was the consequence of poor training as a child, and unwholesome present attitudes on the part of his mother.

The lad was the only son of a widowed mother who had poured out her possessive affections upon him. From early childhood he had been pampered, but the mother's love was selfish rather than self-giving. She had demanded and received constant attention and concern. He had never achieved and, if she had her way, never would achieve independence. His whole life revolved around hers, meeting her wishes, responding to her demands. She lavished upon him gifts and love, but in return required of him his soul.

Now the army had taken him from her, and her resentment was bitter and deep. He was in a small unit which had to develop a high degree of effective team-work. Not only the efficiency of the group, but the very lives of its members, depended upon each man being able to do his job quickly and perfectly. Months of gruelling training were required which could not be broken by furloughs. Each man was required to be on the job all the time until the training period was completed. And he was not pampered in the process either.

But the lad was terribly distracted. He might have become accustomed to the strict discipline and hardships of the Army even though they did contrast so widely with the ease and comfort in which he had been reared, if he had received any encouragement from home. But the opposite was the case. His mother wrote him daily, sometimes two or three letters a day, and frequently wired him. She was terribly lonesome, she told him. She couldn't live without him. Why couldn't he get a furlough? John Jones and Bill Smith, both of whom were inducted later than he, had been home. Why couldn't he come? Didn't he care what happened to his mother? She suspected that he didn't want to come home, and was just finding excuses for staying in camp. Maybe someone had come between them. Life wasn't tolerable without him, and if he didn't come home soon she'd find some way out. And it would be his fault.

Was it any wonder that this young man, reared in ease and luxury, emotionally dependent upon his mother as she was emotionally dependent upon him, terribly disturbed about what might happen to her, was unable to eat, sleep or do his work, or that he was on the verge of serious mental disorder? Persons reared as this young man was reared, who have never achieved autonomy but remain emotionally dependent upon self-centered and possessive parents, are totally unfitted to meet the responsibilities and stresses of life.

Fortunately, only a small proportion of parents adopt such possessive attitudes toward their children as to hinder their emancipation and render them inadequate for the tasks of life. A paragraph in a letter written from overseas by a Red Cross hospital worker to her parents during the war said:

I have taken on the job of letter writing for the boys who can't write. It's quite an experience to sit next to a bed where a boy lies in a traction splint and listen and watch as he begins dictating slowly. Most of the letters begin . . . "Dear Mom" . . . then he has to stop and tell you that she's the best Mom in the world. You get a picture of Mom . . . she's every mother you ever knew, loving her kids, wondering, waiting for word from far away, worrying. And the kid says . . . "Don't worry, Mom, I'm all right. Don't worry because someone else is writing this for me. In a few days, as soon as I can sit up, I'll write myself" . . . So you write the letters, and other boys in other beds, casts and splints closing hard and clean around them, say . . . "Hey, Red Cross, how about writing a letter for me?" So you come back to write another letter . . . "Dear Mom" . . .

Men who can face the stresses and tragedies of life in that manner and out of the depths of their own bitter fate reach out a hand of courage and strength to their loved ones, have been so reared as to be sure, on the one hand, of their parents' love and concern but, on the other hand, they have had nurtured in them a sense of their own responsibility for the management of their lives. They have grown up with a sense of inner emotional security and have achieved adult independence. They are competent members of society.

The training of a child, it must always be remembered, in his fundamental concepts, his basic attitudes and his emotional responses, is chiefly in the hands of his parents, and in our culture that means preponderantly in the hands of mothers. And it is in the early formative years that the fundamental patterns are established and set. If this task of nurture of the mental and emotional life is not accomplished early, the child will almost inevitably be permanently handicapped. It is the old story of striking the iron while it is hot. The iron quickly cools, and when it does the pattern is set. The Scriptural injunction represents a sound psychological insight: "Train up a child in the way he should go, and when he is old he will not depart from it."

For the proper training of a child there are three things which it is important always to remember. They are, first, that the driving forces of human life are emotional, rather than intellectual, and that, therefore, conditions which will favor a healthy emotional life must be provided. Second, that those who would undertake the training of children must have clearly defined goals, particularly with regard to the fundamental character traits they wish to establish.

And, third, that for the transmission of these character traits, a friendly environment is essential. Let us examine these important concerns for the parent and teacher.

First, then, with regard to the primacy of emotion as the driving force of human life, it may be said that there are few things upon which psychologists of all schools are more universally agreed. Man is a thinking animal, as Aristotle said, but he is an acting animal first, driving forward under the propulsion of self-preservative and race-preservative impulses. Thinking is a tool to guide action. When overt behavior is suspended because of the failure of impulse to achieve its object there takes place a dramatic rehearsal in consciousness of possible alternative courses of action by which the objective may be achieved; or the possible substitution of some other objective to satisfy the need may be considered. This is thinking. And it is always the servant of action undertaken to meet the need of the individual whose powerful emotional drives clamor for satisfaction. Man is seldom as rational as he thinks he is. His wants, with their clamorous emotional content, drive him on, and he uses his mind to secure the satisfaction of these wants. Sometimes, indeed, he may use his mind to explain to himself why he does what he does, when the real emotional motivation is something which he does not care to acknowledge. This, of course, is not rationality, but rather what the psychologist calls "rationalization."

It is these emotional drives, then, that must be guided. And it is not so much by formal education or verbal instruction that they are guided. Children are guided by the influence upon them of the primary groups in which they are involved, the first and most important of which is the family. The ideals, attitudes, notions, structures of value, etc., are transmitted to the child in the same manner as language is transmitted. The child does not grow up to be a Christian or a Buddhist or a Mohammedan because he has become convinced that the particular religion he adopts gives the most intelligent answers to the problems of life, but because Christianity, Buddhism or Mohammedanism is the religion believed and practiced by his family. Likewise he grows up truthful, honest and generous, or, on the other hand, mean, vicious and selfish, not because he has been intellectually convinced that those are the ways that will bring him the greatest satisfactions, but because those are the patterns of conduct which have been set for him by his primary group.

This statement is, of course, an over-simplification, although it is basically true. For the process of character formation is an exceedingly complex one. The child does not simply respond automatically to and copy the behavior patterns set him; he responds, rather, in ways that he learns will gain him the satisfactions he wants. Love for his parents may be transformed to resentment and hate, trust may be changed to fear and anxiety, if he finds his wishes constantly frustrated; spontaneous and independent action may be deformed into over-dependence or withdrawal if he is overly pampered or violently inhibited. The point is, it is in the subtle relationships existing in the primary group and especially in the relationships obtaining between parent and child that the fundamental character traits and patterns of emotional reaction are set.

What the wise parent will want for his child is not simply that he inherit unchanged the systems of ideas, structures of value, and points of view cherished in the family, but that he become a creative member of society, able to use his own mind and contribute something to the progress of mankind. This will require that the child shall learn increasingly to bring his conduct under control of intelligence and an enlightened conscience, and not either follow automatically patterns that are set for him or live as the mere creature of impulse. If this is to be accomplished, there are two conditions that the parents must provide. And these are, first, example, and second, freedom.

The second essential element in the training of a child is that there must be clearly defined goals toward which we wish to have the child move. The problem of education is that of the effective transmission of our culture to the oncoming generation, and this cannot be done well unless we have clearly in mind those elements of our culture which we wish to transmit. A man training a hunting dog knows what he wants to accomplish. We should certainly know equally well what we want to accomplish; and also get clearly in mind the methods by which those ends can be achieved.

The human child is the most educable individual on earth. He is capable of being fitted into an infinite variety of cultural molds. The child of the wildest savages, reared in a Christian environment, is as capable of achieving the noblest Christian character as the child of generations of Christians. The most fanatical and cruel Moslems were the Janissaries, the captured children of Balkan Christians trained as shock troops in the Turkish army. Do we want our children to be kind, honest, generous, tolerant? Then we must train them in that direction.

Sometimes progressive education has gone much too far in assuming that a child left to his own devices will grow up into a happy and useful man. This movement was a necessary reaction from the authoritarianism and excessive restrictions of earlier formal education. The child's interests and curiosity must be laid hold upon, and a large measure of freedom permitted and encouraged if he is to enjoy healthy growth. But that does not mean that we should have no goals in the educational process, or lack confidence in the values we seek to transmit. Our values are not rigid and final, and we shall hope our successors will achieve higher goals; but our values are, after all, the deposit of long experience and testing in a creative process which is still going on and into which we wish to initiate our successors. They can only become creative participants in this process if they share and appreciate these values which we now possess. If that is not accomplished our Christian culture and our whole structure of Christian values will die.

And, as has been said, it is within the intimacy of the primary group, and particularly in the free-flowing personal relationships of the family, that these values are transmitted. If, then, the parents wish their children to believe something, they themselves must be believers; they must believe that there is something to live for, something worthy to command their highest allegiance. They must believe in honesty, the love of truth, devotion to duty, courage, loyalty, faith in a goodness based on the will of God, if they wish their children to possess these characteristics. Mere verbalizing will have little value. Children have an extraordinary ability to sense what their parents deeply believe and live by; they cannot be fooled with words. The unfortunate thing is that so many parents have no deep commitments, no basic convictions, no real faith in a living God. Parents whose only concerns are trivialities, whose guide in life is materialistic opportunism, can hardly transmit to their children a robust faith in eternal verities.

The third essential element in the training of children is the provision of a friendly environment. Love is a prime essential in the successful rearing of children. Psychological investigation has established beyond all question the child's need for affection. The child needs the mother's fondling and demonstration of love for the development of its emotional life as much as it needs food for the nourishment of its body. There is abundance of clinical evidence that the unloved child grows up emotionally insecure and that, deprived of love, it almost inevitably responds with hostility and fear. A child needs strong parental figures with whom it feels secure. Parents loving their children, and setting them a worthy example, will find their children following in their steps.

Bishop William Croswell Doane once wrote a little poem

of complaint when, for supposed hygienic reasons, he was not allowed to play with his grandchild:

"The hand that rocks the cradle"—but today there's no such
   hand.
It is bad to rock the baby, they would have us understand;
So the cradle's but a relic of the former foolish days
When mothers reared their children in unscientific ways;
When they jounced them, and they bounced them, those poor
   dwarfs of long ago——
The Washingtons, and Jeffersons, and Adamses, you know!

Another breed of scientists than the hygienists are now having their say—the psychiatrists. And they are telling mothers that to deprive their children of warm evidences of affection is to do them far greater harm than any "bugs" are likely to accomplish.

But it is important that the affection be real, not a façade of affection which has as its real motive the desire to control, to dominate, to receive more in return than is given. "Love seeketh not its own." Reinhold Niebuhr, in his *Interpretation of Christian Ethics*,[1] has spoken a penetrating word. He says:

The most terrific social conflicts actually occur in intimate communities in which the intensity of social cohesion accentuates the social distance of various groups and individuals. Even in the most intimate community, the family, parental, conjugal and filial affection is no perfect guarantee of justice and harmony. All these forces of natural sympathy may become

[1] From *The Interpretation of Christian Ethics*, p. 125, by Reinhold Niebuhr. Copyright by Harper & Brothers and quoted by permission.

façades behind which the will-to-power operates. Even when it is less pronounced than the imperialism of groups it may be more deadly for operating at such close range.

Lack of discipline, lack of well-organized habit systems established on high ethical levels, is too characteristic of our day. Too many children are poorly trained. But the necessary training will not be accomplished by severe and autocratic methods; such methods are largely negative and self-defeating. Verbal "do's" and "don'ts" accomplish little, and severe punishment arouses only rebellion. The child wants to be an accepted member of a group whose other members he admires, and will voluntarily conform to the standards of that group in order to be accepted. Here the family is the most effective educator. If the parents know what virtues they wish to establish in the life of the child and themselves live by them, if they will hold their children in bonds of warm affection, they will mold them in that pattern. It is the positive and constructive attitudes that matter. Repressive and punitive methods will produce only a sham and reluctant conformity, or, even more probably, angry rebellion. And the coercive power is compounded out of the love of the parents, on the one hand, and the powerful urge of the child to deserve approval and to find companionship, on the other.

The responsibilities, then, which parents bear, represent a real call to a three-fold commitment.

First, there is a call to commitment to the moral values we would see realized in our children. Such a commitment is utterly unavoidable. The only way in which we can recommend goodness is by giving our own lives in devotion to that which is good. All else is sham, and the children will know it. If we worship wealth or power or pleasure our children will know that these are our gods, and no words of ours will convince them otherwise. If integrity, courage, truthfulness, kindness and unselfishness characterize our daily lives, our children will know that those are the things we believe in. And they, too, will feel their coercive power.

Second, there is a call to commitment to the welfare of our children. But the devotion must be genuinely to our children and not, under a subtle subterfuge, to ourselves. We must seek their good and not our own. If, by use of a show of devotion, we really seek personal gratification, or the fulfilment of our own frustrated ambitions, or to become the center of their concern, we really hate them and love only ourselves. But genuine love, linked with wisdom, will enable us to train up our children in the way they should go.

And, third, there is a call to commitment and devotion to God, the Father of all mankind, if we would fulfil our duties as human parents in the rearing and training of our children. For it is His will that we seek to know, the doing of which is our highest good. It is as our children learn and do His will that their lives will find their highest fulfilment. And it is within the bonds of the loving family, even more than in church, that faith in God is mediated.

"Faith is a *family* affair," said a recent full-page advertisement placed by the Institute of Life Insurance in 375 daily newspapers and some of the magazines of national circulation. "Children naturally turn to faith when it is a daily part of family life," it went on to say. "The home atmosphere is far different when a family stops trying to walk alone, when it sees its place in the bigger scheme of things. It works together for the things it can control—and trusts its God for guidance in problems beyond its control. Such a family can't help feeling closer together, more sure of itself, happier."

A few years ago there was chosen as Golden Rule Mother a woman whose three sons have risen to high places as scientists and educators, all of them now university presidents, all of them socially-minded public servants, and all of them men of devout religious life. Years before she was chosen for this honor one of the sons told his pastor about a motto engraved inside his mother's wedding ring. The words inscribed were: "Each for the other, and both for God." As the family grew, the motto, and the genuine commitment, of all the members became: "Each for the other, and all for God." Is it any wonder that such a family should produce such sons?

CHAPTER 2

What Makes You "You"?

It matters not how strait the gate,
How charged with punishments the scroll,
I am the master of my fate:
I am the captain of my soul.

So wrote Henley in his poem *Invictus*.

Those are brave words. But how far are they true? How far is one dependent for what he is, not upon his own choices and decisions, but upon his ancestry and environment? We have all heard of the self-made man who was very proud of his maker. But no man has ever appeared on earth who was responsible for his own biological or cultural inheritance. Those elements are not self-made. What a man is physically and in general mental capacity is largely determined by parents, grandparents, and great-grandparents which he did not choose. And, culturally, he is "heir of all the ages' gain." He did not create the language he speaks, the ideas he entertains, nor the structure of values which command his loyalty. He has, of course, done some picking and choosing among these ideas and values, but they are all part of the accumulated treasure of the race of which he is now the happy inheritor. So, the question: "What makes you 'you'?" is a very relevant one.

Yet I shall venture to say that, to a very great extent, even after making full allowance for what both nature and nurture have bestowed, a man is indeed arbiter of his own fate, and captain of his soul. His choices and decisions do determine his destiny.

There can be, of course, no question concerning the importance of heredity. We all are familiar with the aphorisms, "He's a chip off the old block," "Blood will tell," "Like father like son," and so on. A stock breeders' slogan is "Breed the best with the best and you'll always have the best." Our hook-noses, bald heads, short or tall statures are inherited, and so are our native mental capacities. Galton's, Thorndike's and Newman's studies of identical twins, separated shortly after birth and growing up in widely different environments, show that they have remained much alike, not only in physical appearance, but also in mental traits. They are so much alike in their hereditary endowment, both being products of one egg, that, in spite of environmental differences, they have developed into practically parallel personalities.

This fact of hereditary characteristics is observable by everybody. I recall watching a baseball player, whose father I had known thirty years earlier, and it seemed almost as if the father were young again and back on the field. The boy batted, handled the ball, and threw exactly like his father. Sometimes one sees undesirable traits reincarnated in much the same way. "He's just like your family!"

I recall hearing a woman say angrily to her husband when they were discussing some misbehavior of their young son.

The Jukes, Kallikaks and Edwardses, of course, are the classic illustrations of the importance of the hereditary endowment in the development of character. Davenport's study of the Jukes family had only recently been completed when I first began to study sociology in college, and the later study of the Kallikaks followed a similar pattern. "Max," the progenitor of the Jukes family, who lived about one hundred and seventy-five years ago near New York City, was mentally defective, lazy, and generally worthless. His two sons married prostitutes. One of them, "Margaret," became known as "the mother of criminals." Two thousand and ninety-four descendants of the Juke sisters have been traced, and of these 1,258 were living in 1915. Sixty-five were listed as "good citizens"; 600 were epileptic or feeble-minded. Many were criminals, indeed, few escaped some entanglement with the law. They were paupers, mental defectives, criminals, prostitutes, drunkards, and even murderers. Indeed, in seventy-five years the State of New York spent a million and a quarter dollars to support their feeble-minded progeny alone, and it would be difficult to estimate the additional costs arising from the crimes they committed and the disease they spread.

In contrast with the Jukes and Kallikaks the descendants of Jonathan Edwards, the great New England preacher and educator, have been studied. And the record is that of a great number of brilliant, versatile, distinguished men—college and university presidents, clergymen, statesmen, jurists, inventors and others. These studies present a remarkable contrast which cannot be overlooked by any student of heredity. Similar studies might be made of other families. The British aristocracy has produced a number of families which, generation after generation, have provided the nation with outstanding leaders. Winston Churchill is a member of the great Marlborough family; the Cecils have produced prime ministers and eminent statesmen literally through the centuries; and so one might go on. And even in America's short history the same phenomena may be noted.

Yet heredity does not tell the whole story. The great families have produced their wastrels—I met some of them years ago as remittance men in Western Canada. And great and outstanding men have come from the most obscure and unpromising stock. There was George Washington Carver, the sickly Negro slave boy, black as coal, who never knew his father or mother, who became one of America's greatest scientists. And there was Charles Steinmetz, the dwarfed, crippled, poor, German immigrant, who almost was refused admittance to the United States because his distorted and frail body, his poverty and lack of friends, made him liable to become a "public charge," but who became "the wizard of Schenectady," chief engineer of the General Electric Company, and one of the giants in harnessing electrical energy. And Abraham Lincoln—who would have thought that the son of a shiftless, restless, unsuccessful laborer and small farmer, born in a wretched cabin in dire poverty near Hodgenville, Kentucky, would become perhaps the greatest of the Presidents of the United States, liberator of the slaves, preserver of the Union, the author of the Gettysburg Address and the Second Inaugural Address—two of the greatest pieces of literature in our language—and certainly one of the truly great men of all time? How often, indeed, do we hear the names of Jesus, Socrates, and Abraham Lincoln linked together.

Heredity, important as it is, cannot do everything. What seems to be true is that where you have close inbreeding of bad stock you get sorry results; where you have good stock, the probabilities are for a good inheritance, but even there the traditional black sheep occasionally appears. The fact is that many strains are to be found in the inheritance of all of us. As George A. Dorsey reminds us in his *Why We Behave Like Human Beings,* "Reckoning three generations to a century, each of us today is entitled to 120,-000,000,000,000 (120 trillion, or 120 million million) lineal ancestors in A.D. 1. They intermarried. At no time has the earth had 120,000,000,000 people much less 120,-000,000,000,000." [1] Which means, of course, that we are all at least 32nd cousins. And there must be some good and some bad in all of us. Most of the *Mayflower* descendants who are so proud of their ancestry probably could count quite as large a number of ancestors from among the Sons and Daughters of the Steerage as from among those who crossed the ocean on the famous ship that bore the Pilgrim Fathers. The encouraging thing is that all the evidence in-

[1] From *Why We Behave Like Human Beings,* p. 112, by George A. Dorsey. Copyright by Harper & Brothers and quoted by permission.

dicates that, given an even chance—that is, if the good and intelligent people will have children—the good and the healthy are dominant and will breed out the evil.

During the past twenty years or so there has been a turning away from an almost exclusive emphasis upon heredity to renewed attention to the significance of environment. It has been pointed out that those persons who have had th advantage of good heredity have usually also had the ad vantage of good environment; and, vice versa, the unfortunate inheritors of bad stock also grew up in bad surroundings. The Edwardses and Jukes will serve to illustrate this. This insight has been supplemented by sociological investigation.

Clifford Shaw's studies of "Delinquency Areas" is one of the most enlightening in this respect. He has shown that in a number of great cities delinquency rates are high— approaching almost twenty-five per cent annually—in the broken-down slum areas of a city, and that they gradually shade off to less than one per cent in the highly favored suburban areas. And it makes no difference how the population changes in these slum areas—it may change from Italian to Polish to Irish to Jewish to Negro, or anything else—so long as it remains slum it produces the delinquent pattern in the behavior of juveniles. And, as these same population elements with increasing prosperity move out to more favored areas, the delinquency rates among their children decrease to correspond with those which previously obtained in these newer and better areas. That is to say, the incidence of delinquency is high where every other sort of pathological social condition obtains—poverty, poor housing, drunkenness, lack of playgrounds, poor schools, etc. While, on the other hand, low delinquency rates are found where the surroundings are healthful—good homes, churches and schools, adequate parks and playgrounds, fresh air and sunshine, and good community spirit. Environment counts heavily.

I know of no study which illustrates this principle so well as Dr. Pauline Young's study of the Molokan community in Los Angeles.[2] Here a primitive religious community which, in Russia, had remained segregated and passed on its *mores* practically unchanged from one generation to another, was transplanted to Los Angeles, and suffered almost unbelievable disintegration. When the community could control the environment, the children grew up loyal to the peculiar religious beliefs and practices of the sect and also maintained its high moral standards of truth-telling, honesty, chastity and loyalty. But, when subjected to the pressures of urban life, with its conflicting standards and practices, the children and young people not only abandoned the queer religious practices of the Molokans but, confused and demoralized by conflicting pressures, abandoned the strict moral code of the group. The tragic result was that, at the time the study was made, the delinquency rate among Molokan youth was the highest in Los Angeles. Where could one find better evidence of the importance of environmental influences? For the same chil-

[2] *The Pilgrims of Russian-Town.* Chicago: University of Chicago Press.

dren and young people, now in trouble with the police, if they had been reared in the former isolated community, untouched by outside influences, would unquestionably have grown up, like their parents, carrying on the old religious practices and maintaining the same strict moral code.

As a matter of fact, we all recognize the importance of environmental influences or we should not be ready to make the sacrifices we do in order to provide our children with a good education and a wholesome social life. We want for them good schools, good churches, clean-minded companions, healthy opportunity for self-expression, well-directed play and recreation, a pleasant community, and every possible incitement to the good life. And we are ready to pay a pretty high price to get these advantages for our children. Sometimes, indeed, we are over-solicitous, but that only shows the high value we place upon providing a wholesome environment for our children whose welfare is our responsibility.

Perhaps a word to parents about their responsibility here is not out of order. It is not enough merely to provide the material conditions of the good life. Nor is it enough to provide children with good schools or even good facilities for religious education. The most important environmental influence playing upon the child is that of his parents and his home. It is the force of example and personal influence that counts for most. Integrity, altruism, devotion to duty and religion, are not taught out of books but out of life. What you are will count most in determining what your child will be. And the question each parent needs ask is, "What, actually, am I transmitting to my children, not by way of precept, but by way of example?" Most parents would like God to be a real Power and Presence in the lives of their children, but that is not likely to happen unless God is a real power and presence in their own lives. As Dean Inge reminds us: "It is quite natural and inevitable that if we spend sixteen hours daily of our working life in thinking about the affairs of this world, and five minutes in thinking about God . . . this world will seem two hundred times more real to us than God." The thing to keep in mind is that the most important aspect of the environment affecting the personality and character development of our children is not the physical, but the social environment; and, to the child, by far the most important element in the social environment is that child's parents—not merely what those parents say, either, but what they are and do.

We have considered the parts played by heredity and environment in the formation of personality—that is, in making you "you." But if only heredity and environment counted, if they were completely determinative of personality, we should all of us be nothing more than automatons; and that, of course, is exactly what a good many people have insisted that we are. Watson's *Behaviorism*, for example, maintains that thesis. A man is only an extraordinarily complex system of conditioned reflexes—his seeming freedom is an illusion.

The observable fact is, however, that the individual does exercise a considerable measure of control over his fate. He is—within limits, it is true—the captain of his soul. Nothing could so completely paralyze all effort for achievement as the conviction that man is the helpless pawn of forces outside himself and his own volition. Even the very young baby makes it known that he has a will of his own—every father and mother has learned how the baby will howl, cry angrily, hold its breath, and cut all kinds of capers to get its way. As the baby gets older and learns from experience in getting along with people—particularly with mother—he learns what to do and what to avoid in order to gain his ends. As he becomes self-conscious, and especially as he begins to master language, he gains rapidly in the power of reflective thought, in the ability to weigh alternatives, to seek more remote rather than immediate satisfactions, and to clarify the goals of his endeavor. He becomes a thinking, choosing, deliberately purposing free agent. He is by no means the passive victim of either heredity or environment. Certainly the organic driving forces are gifts which heredity bestows. And the goals he seeks are those made available to him by his physical and social environment. But the emerging self is a real factor in the situation, and the choices he makes have real significance in the shaping of his growing and maturing personality. And this process goes on all through life. Increasingly the individual himself is responsible for what he becomes.

Soren Kierkegaard, the Danish philosopher and theologian, used to tell this story: Once there was a wild duck, used to the trackless freedom of the wilderness of the air. On one of his migrations north he chanced to alight in a farmyard where the tame ducks were being fed. He ate some of their corn, and liked it so much that he lingered until the next meal, and the next month, until autumn came and his old companions flew over the farmyard and gave their cry to him that it was time to be away. The old ecstasy of free flight aroused within him again, and he flapped his wings in order to join them, but he could not leave the ground. He had grown fat on the farmer's corn and the indolent life of the barnyard. He resigned himself to remain there, and each season, until his death, the calls of his fellows roused him—but each year the calls seemed fainter and farther away. The wild duck had become a tame duck.

Well, some people are like that. They make choices which ultimately bind them with inner chains. But, at any rate, they once were free to choose. Unfortunately they chose immediate gratifications rather than more remote but loftier fulfilments. And now, any choices they make are, because of previous choices, kept within circumscribed limits. Perhaps this is an overstatement, but it is practically true, as we shall see when we come to discuss "habit." Yet, after all, a man is not a duck, either a wild or a tame one. And stimulations may come that will release unsuspected energies and, even if he has been loafing in the barnyard for a long time, he may yet again penetrate the skies.

It is pretty hard to convince a man, on the basis of some doctrinaire position, that he is not free in his choices. His own inner experience tells him that he is free and responsible. And he has seen that men who have chosen badly have gone on their way to their doom, while men who have chosen wisely, and have directed their energies to the achievement of well-chosen goals, have gone on to successful and useful lives, sometimes in spite of terrific handicaps.

We spoke earlier of George Washington Carver. Few men have ever faced greater handicaps or achieved greater distinction in their chosen fields. Born a sickly baby of a slave mother on a southern plantation—no one knows exactly when except that it was in the early days of the Civil War—he was stolen by night-riders, together with his slave mother, and carried off to Arkansas. A party of searchers found the boy, but the mother already had been sold and was never heard of again. Moses Carver, owner of the plantation from which the slaves had been stolen, bought the boy back—more out of pity for the sickly, scrawny youngster than with any hope that he would grow up to be an economic asset—by exchanging him for a wind-broken horse. When the slaves were set free the Carvers adopted the little fellow and, when he grew old enough, set him to work doing kitchen chores, since he was not strong enough for work in the fields. But, although he became an excellent kitchen helper, he was not content to remain one. He was driven by avid curiosity to wander in the woods, where he gained an intimate acquaintance with insects and animals, plants and flowers and, when he found a dog-eared spelling book, he learned to read. The struggle for an education was a hard one but, despite the handicaps of sickness, poverty and color, his singleness of purpose and intellectual distinction carried him through the grades, high school, college and graduate university work, until he finally was appointed to a professorship in Iowa State College. From there he went to Tuskegee Institute, in Alabama, where he felt that he could be of the greatest service to his own people, and in that institution he gained his great fame. His researches in soil chemistry, in the utilization of such humble products of the soil as peanuts and sweet potatoes, made him one of the greatest economic benefactors of the entire South, white as well as black, and, indeed, of the whole world. In fact, it was not his own country, but Great Britain, which first recognized his greatness in making him, in 1916, a Fellow of the Royal Society for the Encouragement of Arts, Manufacture, and Commerce. But his own country came to recognize him in due time. The Daughters of the Confederacy honored him with a "written expression of their interest and appreciation." The *Birmingham News* said: "Dr. Carver is one of Alabama's most distinguished citizens. The citizens of this State may be proud of him." And, at his death, President Franklin D. Roosevelt wired Tuskegee Institute: "The world of science has lost one of its most eminent figures and the race from which he sprang an outstanding member in the passing of Dr. Carver. The versatility of his genius, and his achievements in diverse branches of arts and sciences were truly amazing. All mankind is beneficiary of his discoveries in the field of agricultural chemistry. The things which he achieved in the face of early handicaps will for all time be an inspiration to youth everywhere."

After his death the United States Post Office issued a commemorative postage stamp in his honor.

Why have I talked so long about George Washington Carver? Simply because he illustrates so well what I have been trying to say. Many other equally illuminating illustrations might have been chosen. What made him what he became? Heredity and environment? Well, viewed objectively, neither was very favorable, although there must have been something in what the biologist calls the "genes," the chemical determinants of personality, to account for his intellectual potentialities and his powerful drives; and there must have been some favorable factors in his environment that stimulated him. But it was, above all, the individual choices, decisions, and dominating purposes of his personality, which overcame every obstacle and handicap, that accounted for his achievement. He was no helpless pawn of Fate. He was "the captain of his soul!"

Or was he? He did, indeed, make his own choices and carve out his own career. But he always felt that he lived under a higher authority. For he was a devoutly religious man. One of his favorite Scripture verses was: "I can do all things through Christ which strengtheneth me." Of his work he said: "Without God to draw aside the curtain I would be helpless. . . . No books ever go into my laboratory. The thing that I am to do and the way to do it come to me. I never grope for methods, the method is revealed to me at the moment I am inspired to do something new. . . ." He regarded himself as an instrument in the hands of God. In expressing his religious philosophy he once said: "It is not we little men who do the work, but it is our blessed Creator working through us." There it is. This great all-encompassing Reality is ready to work through us. But He will not work through automatons. We must be willing to become the channels of His creative power.[3]

What makes you "you"? Heredity? Well, heredity has much to do with it, and we should certainly do all that we can to encourage the abler and more successful people to have more children. It is manifest racial delinquency for those who possess valuable inherited traits which may be passed on to the next generation to evade this obligation. Of course heredity matters. And environment also matters. When considering the part environment plays in the nurture of our children we probably should act as if it were the only thing that did matter, for it is the only thing we can now control. Heredity has done its job, for good or ill. The school, the community, the church, the generally accepted social standards—all these are immensely important. And especially the home, in which the child lives in the company of parents of integrity, good-will, courage, and genuine religion, exercises an unsurpassed influence.

But the personal choice and decision of the individual is, after all, the final determinant. We must do all that we can to guide that decision wisely in all those whom we may influence. If the individual can feel, as Dr. Carver felt,

---

[3] For most of the information concerning Dr. Carver I am indebted to Basil Mathews' book *George Washington Carver*, published by the Zondervan Publishing House, Grand Rapids, Michigan.

that God has a purpose for his life, and that life's true meaning and fulfilment will be found as that purpose is discovered and accomplished, then the "you" that is developed will be worthy, whether or not eminence is achieved. For God Himself is helped or hindered in the accomplishment of His task by our willing coöperation, or lack of it.

Perhaps you will recall George Eliot's poem, in which she describes Stradivarius, maker of violins, as saying:

> "When any master holds
> 'Twixt chin and hand a violin of mine,
> He will be glad that Stradivari lived,
> Made violins, and made them of the best.
> . . . For while God gives them skill
> I give them instruments to play upon,
> God choosing me to help Him. . . .
> . . . If my hand slacked
> I should rob God—since He is fullest good——
> Leaving a blank instead of violins.
> . . . He could not make
> Antonio Stradivari's violins
> Without Antonio."

What makes you "you"? A great variety of forces, your own choice and decision prominently among them. But, if you will submit yourself to that great Goodness, that all-encompassing Power, that Will and Purpose which throbs through the universe—that is to say, to God, in Whom we live and move and have our being—He will make you what you ought to be.

CHAPTER 3

The Art of Growing Up

How OFTEN HAVE we heard a mother say to her six- or seven-year-old child, when he began to cry or scream for something he wanted, "Oh, don't be a baby!" The conduct that seemed appropriate enough in the baby— although we hoped that even the baby would soon get over it—seemed quite inappropriate in an older child. Yet, how much more so in the grown adult!

"When I became a man, I put away childish things," said the Apostle. But how many of us, mature men and women, have followed the Apostle's example? "O, mother, act your age!" a young woman was overheard to say to her mother at a restaurant table. Something had gone wrong with the service, and the plump, over-fed matron seemed about to burst into tears. "Don't mind mother," the girl said to her somewhat embarrassed young man escort. "Mother has always been babied, and I don't think she'll ever grow up!" A bit hard-boiled and inconsiderate? Probably. But there was undoubtedly much truth in what the daughter said.

Multitudes of people fail to "act their age." I once worked for a man who was always "like a bear with a sore head" when things didn't go exactly to suit him. His behavior was infantile. The woman who sulks when she can't have her way, the boy who "won't play" when he can't dominate the game, the husband whose wife "doesn't understand him," the paunchy Legionnaire trying to recapture his youth by boisterous behavior at the annual convention—all these typify those regressions to infantile behavior that may be so easily observed in our friends—but less easily in ourselves. To us it seems quite natural that we should react that way when things go wrong. Said the nurse to the young husband visiting the hospital, "Your wife has been delirious all day, calling for you and crying for money." "Delirious!" replied the husband. "You're mistaken, she's not delirious. Thank heaven, she's back to normal!" Normal, perhaps, but infantile.

Most people grow up physically although, due to glandular failure, a few unfortunate people remain permanently dwarfed. Most people grow up mentally, although to varying intellectual statures, but a few unfortunates remain dwarfed in this respect, too. A much larger number of people, however, fail to grow up in ways that are not so easily observable—they remain emotionally immature. Indeed, all of us, probably, have our infantile regressions. We react to difficult and trying situations with emotions and patterns of behavior which we learned as children would get results from our indulgent parents, but which are inappropriate to grown men and women.

Perhaps we should stop for a little while to inquire as to what is the nature, and what are the roots, of infantilism;

and also to inquire into the nature of that maturity which we have a right to expect of grown people. What are the "childish things" which a man should "put away"? What attitudes and behavior are appropriate to one who has "become a man"?

Infantilism can be separated into two main elements. First, self-centeredness—an egoistic striving for gratification of personal needs without consideration of other persons; and, second, patterns of behavior by means of which the child learned that he could secure the things he desired from others. Many of these forms of behavior had to be curbed early—such as temper tantrums, holding the breath, screaming, and so on. But when the parents, instead of being wise, were indulgent, and would do anything to keep the youngster from raising the roof, the behavior, of course, was continued. This sort of conduct, difficult to endure, but still perhaps bearable in a child, is intolerable in an adult. Yet it is precisely this form of behavior, in more subtle forms perhaps, that many adults continue in order to gain their ends. They weep, they fall sick, they demand attention, they sulk, they bully, they do any one of a score of things that they found useful as babies in getting what they wanted. And all of them are infantilisms.

Now, this self-centeredness, in a baby, is perfectly normal, and is, indeed, essential to its survival. The baby is a bundle of biological needs—needs for food, for warmth, for shelter, for affection—and if it did not make its needs known they might easily be forgotten and the baby would not survive. You can't expect altruism in a baby. Altruism is something that looks toward the preservation of the race, but the baby is solely concerned with the preservation of one individual—himself. Altruism is something that has to be learned by the growing child, and should become dominant in the adult. The entire preoccupation of the baby, however—and quite properly so—is with the gratification of his own individual needs.

But the ways in which the child most effectively makes its wants known, and so secures the satisfaction of its needs, are learned. The wise mother who responds intelligently to the child's needs, who sees that the baby is regularly fed, is kept comfortable and warm, and given such evidence of affection that it feels secure, will, if the baby is well, almost certainly have a well-behaved child. If, however, she is either neglectful or over-solicitous, she may find her child quickly becoming a problem. If yelling or temper brings rewards, yelling and temper will become the established behavior pattern. Further, if the mother shows anger or passion in her relations with the child, the child will almost inevitably respond in the same manner. Such behavior patterns, once established, go on in the life of the growing child and, too often, are continued into adult life. I once saw a very little girl angrily tucking her doll in its carriage, slap it in the face and say, "Shut up, damn you!" Where did she learn that? It is easy to guess. And, unfortunately, it boded ill for the developing character of the child.

Now, growing into maturity is, first, outgrowing this infantile self-centeredness and, second, developing patterns of behavior appropriate to the achievement of goals larger than mere self-gratification which the mature individual will set for himself. To achieve this goal of maturity should be the endeavor of each one of us. It is quite all right for a child to speak as a child, to understand as a child, and to think as a child, but when one becomes a man he should put away childish things.

Let us, then, look at the process by which maturity is achieved. One suffers a good many growing pains in becoming adult, and there is danger of fixation at almost any point when the challenge of an expanding world seems too great. But there are almost limitless possibilities of growth if we will have it so. Few of us achieve the stature that we might reach. Fuller, richer, more liberated life always beckons as long as we live and, perhaps, will do so eternally. That may be the meaning of eternal life.

Becoming mature, then, as has been said, means, in the first place, growing out of infantile self-centeredness. There is nothing blameworthy in a baby being self-centered, but there is much that is blameworthy and in every way damaging in an adult being self-centered. A doctor, writing from a military hospital, said, "I've seen self-pity and infantilism in many men in this war, and it is not the combat shock, but the personality inadequacy, that unfits and destroys them for normal life after their return from overseas." And it is, of course, this infantilism, this vast self-concern, that unfits so many people for their responsibilities in every walk of life.

Growth, maturation, means moving out of oneself into

ever-expanding circles of living. It means entering richly into and sharing the lives of other persons. It means sympathy, coöperation, participation. Basil Mathews, in his *Clash of Color*, tells of standing with the sports captain of a college, who was training a team of boys drawn from all parts of the world. "What special difficulty do you find in training a team like this?" he asked. "A real hard nut to crack," the captain replied, "is just this. These fellows come from countries where the whole idea of team play is unknown. Each, at the beginning of his football training, wants to dribble the ball down the field at his own feet and score the goal himself for his own glory. So, I have won the battle, not only for the boy as a member of the team, but for his whole life-job, when I have *taught him to pass*." [1]

The normal process of growth to maturity, then, is precisely this expansion of the self to include not only one's own individual interests but also the interests and concerns of other people. In a good home the child soon learns to consider the rights and happiness of brothers and sisters; later, concern for the community develops, then the nation, and finally all men. We are told to "love our neighbors as ourselves," and the neighbor, in Jesus' teaching, turns out to be not just the person next door—he may be the hitherto hated alien. But the interesting thing is that one finds that he is not thinking merely of the interests of other persons as over against his own, in order that he may achieve a nice balance and so love his neighbor in exactly the same

[1] From *The Clash of Color*, p. 111, by Basil Mathews, by permission of the Friendship Press.

degree as he loves himself. By a sort of empathy he enters into and shares the lives of others and, as he does so, his whole personality expands and enriches, so that the welfare of the whole becomes a matter of much greater concern than merely his own individual welfare. Thus parents readily sacrifice themselves for their children's happiness, the patriot is ready to sacrifice even life itself for his country, thousands of doctors have risked their lives in dangerous research to discover the causes of disease that ravaged their fellow-men, and not a few have actually given their lives, missionaries have gone to the ends of the earth and endured untold hardship to take knowledge, health, and the light of the Gospel to those who sat in darkness. Of all these, soldiers and civilians, who so identified themselves with their fellow-men that even their individual survival seemed of small moment, it may be said, as Pericles said of the Athenian warrior dead, "Their glory survives in everlasting remembrance. . . . Far away in alien lands their memory is set in the hearts of men." One may so completely identify himself with a larger whole as to merge himself into it, losing himself, yet realizing himself on higher levels. Sang Rupert Brooke, that gallant young soldier and poet who gave his life in the First World War:

> If I should die, think only this of me:
> > That there's some corner of a foreign field
> That is forever England.[2]

[2] Reprinted from *The Collected Poems of Rupert Brooke,* published by Sidgwick & Jackson, Ltd. By permission of the Literary Executors of Rupert Brooke. Copyright, 1915, by Dodd Mead & Co.

Those who thus find themselves caught up in and merged with the larger community, so that their petty affairs matter little, and the welfare of the whole is everything, have learned the profound secret of that strange paradox of Jesus, "He that loseth his life . . . shall find it."

Maturity, in other words, means the ability to stand outside one's narrow self, as it were, and to judge persons and events, not in terms of ego-centric, individual self-interest, but in terms of the common good. It means achieving freedom from personal bias and prejudice and expansion into a larger whole. Such an expansion represents no diminution or narrowing of life. One who achieves it finds himself a pulse in a larger life. He is one of those who indeed "have life, and have it more abundantly."

But the art of growing up requires not only the expansion of the self so that the interests of other persons, rather than narrow self-interest, become dominant; it requires also that these larger and farther goals that are now sought be striven for in mature ways.

Petulance, sulking, day-dreaming, temper, can have no part in truly adult behavior. What is required is unbiased, objective appraisal of the demands of the situation, and intelligent behavior directed to the achievement of the goals sought. Sentimentality will not do. We must not merely imagine how lovely everything would be if things were thus and so; we must put some muscle, perhaps some genuinely sacrificial endeavor, into making them thus and so. Wish-thinking never creates a world nearer to heart's desire.

In his book *The Return to Religion*, Henry C. Link, an

eminent psychotherapist, says: "Hundreds of people have told me, 'Yes, I believe in some kind of a God, or Divine Being, but not in an orthodox way. I don't belong to a church because the formal doctrines and practices of the church and its members are repugnant to me.' There was a time when I would nod in sympathy with such a declaration, it fitted so well my own agnosticism and withdrawal from the church. Now I realize that this attitude was often a symptom of similar attitudes in other realms of life. My clients believed in friendship, for example, but not in the social activities and personal sacrifices by which friends are made. They believed in a happy marriage, but not in the many acts by which it is achieved. They believed in their abilities and aptitudes, but not in the routine drudgery by which superiority in any vocation is attained." [3]

There you have it said excellently. Impulsive behavior, sentimental day-dreaming, are not enough to gain mature goals. Careful thought and planning, objectivity, and perhaps a good bit of real self-sacrifice, will be required to achieve genuinely adult behavior. Do you recall the words of Socrates to his judges, when, on trial for his life, he could easily have saved himself by a slight sacrifice of what he considered the demands of virtue? "A man who is good for anything ought not to calculate the chances of living or dying; he ought only to consider whether he is right or wrong."

A terrific storm was raging off the coast of New England

[3] From *The Return to Religion*, p. 20, by Henry C. Link. Copyright 1936 by The Macmillan Company and used with their permission.

and the coast-guard boat was preparing to put out to the relief of a distressed vessel. One of the young seamen protested to the coast-guard captain, "The tide is moving out, and the wind is offshore. We can go out, but we can never return." To which the captain replied, "We have to go out; but we do not have to return!" There you have represented the sense of devotion to duty, of loyalty to the larger-than-self, which characterizes genuinely adult behavior.

Probably such mature attitudes require an undergirding philosophy of life which is essentially religious. For maturity involves identification of one's self with a larger group, in which one's individual concerns are lost in the values of the larger group, so that one's motivations are not derived from individual self-interest, but from the good of the whole. Religion represents utter devotion to that ultimate good, which is conceived as the will of God. That is, indeed, the very heart of religion—a sense of supreme value which outstrips all individual values, a joyous self-dedication of life to God and His purposes for human life. Thus one may, indeed, lose himself on lower levels of self-gratification, but find himself on higher, nobler, larger levels of self-realization.

One may find many examples of the mature life, but the supreme exemplification of maturity that has appeared in history is Jesus Christ. He grew, we are told, "in wisdom and stature, and in favor with God and man." Of course, as a baby, he possessed the same cravings for the satisfaction of his individual needs as do all other babies, and he, no doubt, manifested them as all babies do. But the fact is that we have no dependable information about him from infancy on through childhood, until he arrived at maturity, except a brief glimpse when he was twelve years of age. We have fables and legends, but they have no historical value, and are quite manifestly products of the pious imagination. But there is evidence that his mother was widowed some time before Jesus began his public ministry, and without doubt as the eldest son responsibilities for the support of the family and care of the younger children fell upon him. Thus, adult responsibilities early became his lot, and he experienced the necessity of considering the family interests before his own. Pious Jewish religion, which exalted the family and called for devotion to God and love of one's neighbor, was undoubtedly a dominant feature of life in his own home. At any rate, when the record begins again, we find a man with a deep sense of responsibility to God and his fellows. His meat, he says, is to do the will of God and to finish His work. But his is not a kind of piety that involves a hermit life and a devotion to God which disregards his fellows. The second command, "Thou shalt love thy neighbor as thyself," is on a level with the first, "Thou shalt love the Lord thy God with all thy heart," and is, indeed, "like unto it." That is, the supreme motivation of Jesus' life is not in the gratification of his own needs but in the service of God and his fellows. That is maturity.

And it was much more than a form of words. Christ's teaching is of immense importance; but what he was is of far more importance than anything he said. For his life exemplified his teaching. He met disappointment, scorn and treachery, but he was never cynical and he never turned aside from his great purpose and mission. He endured bitter cruelty and pain, but there was no resentment or self-pity. He was deserted and left alone, at times it seemed not only by men but by God, but his faith held fast. That bitter cry on the cross, "My God! My God! why hast Thou forsaken me?" echoes down through the ages, and has been echoed in the hearts of multitudes of suffering souls who have felt themselves utterly deserted. But he knew, at last, that bitter as was his lot, he was not deserted. His last words on the cross were, "Father, into Thy hands I commend my spirit." And his faith was justified. For his life and his death have brought salvation to millions. His was that complete maturity which merged his life with all mankind, sharing their burdens, carrying their sorrows, and working their redemption. "Surely he hath borne our griefs and carried our sorrows. . . . He was wounded for our transgressions, he was bruised for our iniquities."

Should we seek this kind of maturity rather than the narrow egoism and self-centeredness of the infant? We shall never achieve it fully, yet "not failure, but low aim is crime." We may well heed the injunction of Phillips Brooks: "Do not pray for easy lives! Pray to be stronger men. Do not pray for tasks equal to your powers. Pray for powers equal to your tasks! Then the doing of your work shall be no miracle. But you shall be a miracle."

And, it might be added, you shall then have grown up!

CHAPTER 4

"Out of the Heart of Man . . ."

IN HIS BOOK *On Being a Real Person*,[1] Dr. Harry Emerson Fosdick tells about the little girl who took a note from her mother to her physiology teacher saying: "Dear Teacher, I don't want my Mary to learn anything more about her insides."

One of the most violent reactions against psychoanalysis in the early days was of just this sort. When the curtain was drawn aside, and people were asked to look at their fundamental motivations, they felt a sort of horror. Clergymen and moralists were especially appalled. Freud's emphasis upon sex motivations in his discussion of the psychodynamics of human behavior was especially distasteful, and many preachers didn't want their parishioners to hear anything more about it. Adler's underscoring of the drive to power was only a bit less unacceptable. Altogether, the "libido" seemed to be a nasty, slimy, wilful thing which, if you avoided looking at it long enough, might cease to exist. Indeed, this underworld of the human psyche was altogether unpleasant. All sorts of wild, tumultuous, passionate, organic hungers and appetites were there clamor-

[1] Harper & Brothers. Used by permission.

42

ing for satisfaction. It just wasn't nice to think of such matters. Let's forget about it and think of lovely things!

But the trouble was that, nice or nasty, these impulses and passions turned out to be the driving forces of human life, and, if ignored or repressed, they nevertheless went on working dynamically in the human psyche with all sorts of unpleasant consequences. Nervous disorders, neurotic symptoms, serious illness, warped conduct which seemed beyond the control of the individual resulted. Or, even if not repressed, these impulses, given free rein, held potentialities of evil. "Out of the heart of man evil thoughts proceed, murders, adultery, fornication." So, what is one to do? If you repress these libidinous drives you get into trouble, and if you let them work their will you are in trouble also. No wonder that out of this unhappy condition many a man has said: "O wretched man that I am!"

But it turns out that this same raw material produces the best and noblest in human life. The sex drive which, misused, may produce the deepest degradation, provides the foundation of the family, with all its mutuality, sharing, love and care. So with combativeness—it is an essential part of our biological equipment if we are to continue to survive in a world where much threatens. Misused, it may bring horror, pain and death to many, as witness the carnage of war. But, properly directed, it may meet and defeat unnumbered foes to human fulfilment.

In short, there is nothing evil about the elemental drives themselves—it is what we do with them, the manner in which we direct them, that makes them good or evil. Was it not Freud himself who said that "civilization is forged at the cost of instinct satisfaction." Civilization would be impossible if men and women sought only the immediate personal gratification of their appetites; it is only as the drive of these impulses is placed at the service of effort to gain higher and more socially useful goals that a civilized life can be achieved. Indeed, the highest achievement of our culture—our art, literature, science, social amenities, the kindness and consideration of men for each other, the altruistic endeavors of great-hearted persons—may all be truly interpreted as sublimations of these powerful inherited biological urges.

Another bit of parent-teacher correspondence is said to have run in this fashion: Johnny was sent home from school with a letter from his teacher which said: "Johnny is very dirty. He smells. Give him a bath." To which the mother replied with another note: "Johnny ain't no rose. Learn him, don't smell him."

Perhaps that is our cue with regard to these libidinous drives, these dynamic elemental impulses. They must be taught and directed, not "smelled" disdainfully. Indeed, that is the answer to the problem raised earlier. Mere repression doesn't kill the drive—it only perverts it and distorts the personality. To yield it uncontrolled gratification issues in evil consequences of all sorts. But to sublimate it, that is to direct it so that it becomes the driving power for activities which will promote the highest ends of human endeavor, is to lift life to ever nobler levels. This is, indeed, what Freud teaches, but because of his emphasis upon the evil consequences of mere repression, it has been too much overlooked. These impulses are neither to be repressed nor given free rein; they are to be sublimated to purposes personally satisfying and socially acceptable. And the whole purpose of the psychoanalytic technique of the exploration of the "unconscious" is to face the patient with his hidden motivations in order that he may be enabled to bring them under the control of intelligence and an enlightened conscience. The steam in a tea kettle will blow it to pieces if the lid and spout are soldered tight, but that same power of steam will drive the vast machines that men have built and lift intolerable burdens from the shoulders of mankind. In the same way biological drives repressed may do untold damage, but harnessed and directed they will bring human life to its truest fulfilment.

But it should not be thought that out of the heart of man *only* evil thoughts proceed. The human heart is also a source of good. Altruism, unselfishness, devotion to noble causes also have their origin there. A man may, as Jesus exhorted, "love the Lord his God *with all his heart.*" We may "set our affections on things above." And the greatest achievements of the human spirit have been accomplished when the heart has thus been set upon the good. So Florence Nightingale led her little band of nurses to care for the frightfully neglected, wounded and sick soldiers of the Crimean War; so Wilberforce and Lincoln, at great cost to themselves, struck the shackles from millions of human slaves; so John Howard travelled about Europe visiting the literal hells upon earth in which criminals were incarcerated, sometimes for very slight offences, and initiated modern prison reform; so David Livingston gave his life to heal Africa's "open sore of the world"; so Jane Addams identified herself as a neighbor with the denizens of Chicago's slums, working with them as a neighbor to better their lot. All these efforts, too, came "out of the heart of man"—out of the hearts of men touched with sympathy, hearts that bore other men's burdens as if they were their own.

From a church of which I was pastor during the First World War a young man went overseas as bugler in the Marine Corps. He was a lad of fine Christian ideals and unselfish life. One Sunday morning in the Men's Class this lad's father told how he and the boy's mother had been praying, "God keep him safe." Then, he told us, they had somehow felt constrained to change their prayer. In the task in which their son was engaged he could not be safe. And they felt compelled to pray, "God make him brave. God keep him true." It was only about two weeks later that they received the fateful telegram from the Secretary of War saying that their son had been killed. Some months afterward the lad's mother showed me some of the letters written by her son from overseas. Although a bugler, he was used, when his outfit was in action, as a messenger when telegraph or telephone communication had broken down. He said in one letter, "I never know what the message contains. It may be a mere routine order, or it may be something that involves the very lives of my friends. But I say a little prayer and do my best to get through. And I always seem to have a strange sense of God's presence on these lonely and dangerous journeys." It was while carrying such a message across a field under heavy shell and machine-gun fire that he joined the company of the glorious dead.

"Greater love hath no man than this, that a man lay down his life for his friends." Whether it be in peace or war, this identification of one's self with one's fellows, so that one counts not even one's life to be dear unto oneself, is the noblest achievement of the human spirit. It is great-heartedness. Out of the heart of man noble thoughts and deeds of unselfish devotion proceed.

The great task in sublimation, then, is to find the goals toward which our human striving should be directed, to discover the values upon which our affections should be set.

And it is here that religion performs its two-fold function. And that function is, first, to set the goals of worthy achievement; and, second, to release in the lives of men the powers necessary for this achievement.

To indicate and make alluring and emotionally compelling the permanent and universal values to which one should give oneself, to present a cause worthy of the utter devotion of men, is precisely what Jesus did. And his word was: "Seek ye first the Kingdom of God, and His righteousness." To discover God's Kingdom and to devote oneself to it is the true goal of all human endeavor.

In his recent important book *Civilization on Trial* Arnold Toynbee insists that the goal of history is nothing less than the Kingdom of God. If men are to be saved, and if civilization is to be saved, men must discover the purpose of God in history and commit themselves to it. And this purpose is, he maintains, a Kingdom which transcends this world, but in which this world may become a province. To work for the coming of the Kingdom of God is the goal that religion sets. This is the supreme loyalty which should command our hearts' devotion.

But to make the ideal of the Kingdom concrete, so that men may understand specifically what is required of them to promote the Kingdom, is a very difficult task. Any attempt to blue-print a plan and program involves setting forth something much less than the ultimate goal, and possibly, indeed, proposals which, in practice, will prove futile and false. Idealistic men and women have tried many utopian schemes which they identified with the Kingdom of God which, in the end, proved to be self-defeating. Nothing less than the Kingdom itself will do as an ideal to command our hearts' allegiance, and it will be mankind's abiding task and challenge to plan and test the means by which that Kingdom shall be advanced. But always the dream and the hope and the faith will move them.

The fact is that it is the great ideals, perhaps never fully realizable, like "liberty, fraternity, equality," "government of the people, by the people, and for the people," "democratic freedom," etc., that possess power to stir the emotions and move men to great endeavor and sacrifice, rather than the details of a political structure or economic plan by which they may be achieved. The task of religion in setting goals which shall command the loyalty of men is to gain commitment to the will of God, and then progressively to discover what that will requires in terms of day-by-day decision. It is such a commitment that gives direction to mankind's dynamic drives and impulses. It is through such a consecration to the Kingdom that a man's heart is set upon righteousness rather than upon evil.

And the further task of religion, besides setting goals, is that of releasing power for the struggle toward those goals. Here, through all the centuries, religion has revealed its unparalleled value. For the unshaken conviction that one labors with God, that one is, indeed, the instrument of a divine purpose, the very organ of Deity, gives one unconquerable power. "It is God which worketh in you, both to will and to do His good pleasure," said the Apostle Paul to the Philippian Christians. And, strong in that conviction, he was able to say: "I can do all things through Christ which strengthened me."

"Out of the heart of man," then, both evil and good proceed, and whether it shall be good or evil depends upon individual decision. The strong driving forces of human nature, represented by the "heart," may be the means of either our damnation or our salvation. The exhortation of the Wise Man, then, is sound: "Keep thy heart with all diligence, for out of it are the issues of life." Let us examine a little more carefully this problem of "keeping the heart," and the difficulties that beset us in the endeavor.

By the "heart," as used here, one does not mean of course the physical organ, but the seat of the motives and desires. It is true that the heart seems to be affected by the emotions, and that, no doubt, is the reason that the term "heart" is used in this figurative sense. "My heart was in my mouth," a frightened person may say; or, "my heart sank" will express disappointment; "my heart was full" may express either sorrow or joy. But other organs may be thus used figuratively. One's stomach may be upset by a disgusting scene, and much Oriental literature speaks, as does the Apostle Paul, of "bowels of compassion." It is of the heart as the source of motivation and desire, then, that we speak when we say that "out of the heart of man" evil or good thoughts and deeds proceed.

If we would "keep our hearts" we must be careful of the heart's deceitfulness. "The heart is deceitful above all things" is not only a phrase from inspired Scripture but is a statement of profound psychological insight. For we undertake to deceive, not others only, but our very selves, with regard to motives for our behavior which, if frankly faced, might cause us shame.

"The white man's burden" was a burden which it is very doubtful if the white man would willingly have carried except for the enormous profits which exploitation of the colored man provided. Yet there is no doubt that in the process of exploitation some benefits were conferred upon the colored races, and these benefits were seen by Kipling as the motivation for the white man's labor. The men who directed the horrible tortures of the Holy Inquisition claimed, and perhaps sincerely believed, that they were moved by concern for the souls of men threatened by heresy; but to us, looking back at it, the real motivation seems much more surely to have been lust for power and wealth. In some degree we probably all deceive ourselves.

A young woman in an Ohio church met a young man who had volunteered for missionary service in the Belgian Congo. She began to inquire about and read up on Christian work among the Congo natives and soon herself became a missionary volunteer. She gave addresses on missionary work before various groups, and was especially concerned about what might be done to build better Christian homes in the Christian communities of the Belgian Congo and provide Christian nurture for the children. She became engaged to the young man who first interested her in missionary service, and plans were made to send them out to the Congo together. But the romance ended, and the young woman's missionary enthusiasm immediately died. She found that she wasn't a bit interested in the "dirty little black heathen." She never really had been, although her own heart probably had deceived her in the matter. Her real motivation was her love for the young missionary. "The heart is deceitful above all things."

Again, if we would "keep our hearts with all diligence" we must beware of the heart's downright wickedness. "The heart is deceitful above all things *and dreadfully wicked.*" What men revealed themselves to be capable of doing during the war years, not only on the field of battle, but even more in concentration camp and torture chamber, set moralists aghast the world around. The utter ruthlessness and heartless cruelty practiced by so-called "civilized" people seemed almost beyond belief. Indeed, many refused to believe events not only fully proved but frankly confessed. It seemed utterly incredible that human beings could be guilty of such hideous cruelties to their fellow-men.

"Original sin" the makers of the creeds called this capacity for wickedness. The psychologists find the source of these evil propensities in our inherited animal impulses and passions. In any case, these tendencies to lust, cruelty, hate, greed and fury, are deep within us, part of our nature over which is spread a too thin veneer of decency. And at times these elemental passions break loose. "The heart is . . . dreadfully wicked." Indeed, this potential wickedness of the heart of man has become such an obsession with post-war theologians that many of them can see nothing but evil in man's original nature.

But, if one will take the word of Jesus as well as the testimony of experience, the heart of man is not altogether and only evil. "A good man out of the good treasure of his heart bringeth forth that which is good; and an evil man out of the evil treasure of his heart bringeth forth that which is evil: for out of the abundance of the heart the mouth speaketh." If, therefore, we would "keep our hearts with all diligence" we should cherish and nurture that which is good and eschew that which is evil. The choice and decision are ours. It is that which prevails in the heart, as Jesus so constantly insisted, that ultimately finds expression in word and deed. And the keeping of the heart is in our care.

Call it "sublimation," call it "Christian consecration," or call it what you will, the fact is that these powerful inherited impulses may be made the instruments of good, the powerful driving forces of a noble life, if properly directed, just as, if allowed to run wild, they may become the instruments of destruction. It is "out of the heart of man" that both good and evil proceed. We may well then, with the Psalmist, pray, "Search me, O God, and know my heart; try me and know my thoughts: and see if there be any wicked way in me; and lead me in the way everlasting."

And the way to "sublimation," to the achievement of wholeheartedness and freedom from the disintegrating inner turmoil of conflicting desire, is that so simply stated by our Master: "Set your affections on things above!" We may determine what we shall think about and what we shall set our affections upon. "Whatsoever things are true, whatsoever things honest, whatsoever things are just, whatsoever things are pure, whatsoever things are lovely . . . *think* on these things." The Apostle does not say *"Do these things!"* he only says, *"Think* on these things!" Let these things fully occupy your thoughts and they will issue in overt conduct for "as a man thinketh in his heart, so is he."

CHAPTER 5

Instinct, Intelligence, and Purpose

PROFESSOR THORNDIKE'S BOOK, *The Original Nature of Man*, had only recently been published when I began the study of educational psychology. The "original" nature of man, driven by a variety of instincts, was shown to be a very different thing from the "acquired" nature of man. "Human nature" in the raw, as he pictured it at any rate, is a very different sort of entity from the human nature which we meet daily in our homes, on the street and, perhaps most particularly, in church.

This problem of the "nature" of human nature is a very old one. The theologians inevitably have wrestled with it. St. Augustine, basing his theory in part on his own terrific struggle with fleshly temptation and in part on the Bible, maintained that man had inherited a nature totally corrupt. The result of Adam's fall from a state of original innocence was so disastrous that all his descendants possessed a nature which, in itself, was totally and universally depraved. Man is utterly incapable of a good act. Of himself he does evil, and only evil, continually. At the other end of the scale are those represented by Pelagius, the great opponent of Augustine, who maintained that the nature of man is essentially good. Men are sons of God, and endowed by their Creator with the capacity of living as sons of God. It is their task and responsibility so to live.

These two views have wrestled with each other down through the ages. In times of optimism and success, when man seemed to be bending the forces of nature to do his will and to bring those forces under control in the service of a good life for man, the Pelagian view has tended to be dominant. In times like the present, following a war, or in any time when the forces of evil seemed to be arrogant and threatening, when human life was insecure, when one became aware of the terrific power of evil and of the helplessness of man in his struggle against those powers, the Augustinian view has tended to prevail.

I remember that when I came to examine the views of the anthropologists, sociologists, and psychologists about human nature, it came as somewhat of a shock to discover that these scientists seemed to be completely oblivious to these interminable theological discussions. They turned from speculation to empirical observation. It reminds one of the story of a group of medieval scholars who were inquiring as to the number of teeth which a horse possessed. But no one knew because the page in Aristotle which contained that information had been torn from the book. One of the scholars, to the horror of the rest, suggested that they look in a horse's mouth. These scientific inquirers about the nature of man began to look at man. They started with man as they found him—the anthropologists by searching the ancient records the archeologists dug up, by an examination of primitive societies, and even by reaching far back into man's pre-human ancestry to discover what sort of creatures and society eventually produced man. The sociologist was interested in man as a member of society, whether primitive, pre-literate, ancient or modern. The psychologist was interested in the intellectual, emotional and volitional life of man, anywhere and at any time. Of course, there was a great deal of overlapping between the investigations conducted in these various fields. While there has been great difference of opinion among students in these fields on matters of major importance, there is substantial agreement that human nature represents the fruition of a long evolutionary process, that the driving forces of human life are instinctual urges closely related to organic processes, that these urges have been modified in their expression through nurture in a maturing social medium, and that in man these instinctual urges may, at least in some degree, be directed by intelligence and purpose.

But where does this leave the old theological and ethical discussions about the "goodness" or "badness" of human nature? Well, most of these scientific investigators would say that human nature in itself is neither good nor bad, moral nor immoral; it is amoral. Goodness and badness are social concepts; they are terms which define behavior in social situations. Morally good conduct is socially approvable conduct; morally bad conduct is socially disapprovable conduct. The possibility of behavior which will be defined as either "good" or "bad" certainly is present in the tendencies of the organism—in original nature, if you will.

The baby quickly discovers this by the responses which his spontaneous behavior receives from his mother and nurse. "Bad," "naughty" are always among the first words of which he learns the meaning. But the impulse itself, apart from the tag which society attaches to its expression, cannot be morally labelled.

To some this will seem to leave God out of the picture altogether. But that by no means follows. If God is the great creative Force, the ethical and spiritual Person who, through all these processes, is molding us according to His will, then that which we come to understand as "good" is His will for human life; that which we designate as "evil" is the conduct opposed to His will. And His purpose will be the true fulfilment of our lives in righteousness and love. Thus, "to be spiritually minded is life and truth."

William Herbert Carruth says it beautifully in his poem:

A fire mist and a planet,
　　A crystal and a cell,
A jelly-fish and a saurian,
　　And caves where the cave-men dwell;
Then a sense of law and beauty,
　　And a face turned from the clod,—
Some call it Evolution,
　　And others call it God.

A picket frozen on duty,
　　A mother starved for her brood,
Socrates drinking the hemlock,
　　And Jesus on the rood;

> And millions who, humble and nameless,
>   The straight, hard pathway plod,—
> Some call it Consecration,
>   And others call it God.[1]

You will have to make up your own mind as to what this long painful process means for you. For some, it is a cold, barren, meaningless, material process, which has, strangely, eventuated in man with all his possibilities of devotion, love and sacrifice; for others, it is God at work in His world and in the heart of man. That conviction is the very soul of all high religion.

Whatever view you may take of the nature of human nature, this, I think, we shall all agree upon—it is necessary that our wayward and discordant impulses be brought under control of intelligence and an enlightened conscience; that a worthy purpose shall command our loyalty so that the driving forces of our lives shall be directed to the good.

And our impulses *are* wayward and discordant. They seem, sometimes, almost to pull us apart. If our personalities were dominated only by impulse we should be like the gallant knight who mounted his horse and rode rapidly in all directions. For the pulls and pushes within us tend in all directions. There is a little verse that reads:

> Within my earthly temple there's a crowd:
> There's one of us that's humble, one that's proud;
> There's one that's broken-hearted for his sins,

[1] From *Each in His Own Tongue,* by William Herbert Carruth. By permission of Mrs. William Herbert Carruth.

And one that, unrepentant, sits and grins;
There's one that loves his brother as himself,
And one that thinks of naught but power and pelf.
From much disturbing conflict I'd be free
If I could once determine which is "me"!

When I was a youngster I sang in an Episcopal Church choir. In our white surplices, singing to the praise of God, I think we choristers must have looked quite cherubic. The priest in charge, however, knew that we had quite other impulses than those which found expression in worship, and made provision for us to sublimate those impulses in a Boys' Boxing Club which operated in the church basement. There everything was kept pretty well under control, but we no longer looked angelic while trying to slaughter each other. Sometimes the fights which started in the basement were finished surreptitiously in the alley, and, there, quite non-ecclesiastical features were added, such as name-calling and swearing and the complete abandonment of the Marquis of Queensberry rules.

What you will notice here is that the conflicting inner impulses—to sing harmoniously in church and to fight ferociously in the alley—are supplemented and supported by social sanctions. In the church the lad wants to make good as a choir boy, to express himself and also to gain social approval; as a scrapper in the alley he also wants to make good, to demonstrate his prowess and to win the applause of his fellows. Now, this desire for approval is also part of human nature. Indeed, it is nurture in the social group by the giving or withholding of approval that has developed *human,* as contrasted with merely animal, nature. But the groups are so many and varied, their codes and "mores" conflict so violently, that it is difficult, if one wishes to be accepted in different groups, to develop a consistent personality. The inner conflict of impulse is accentuated by the conflict between the standards of the groups in which, at different times, we find ourselves. This somewhat amusing tendency of the choir boy to be an angel in church but a young devil in the back alley becomes serious when carried into adult life; that is, when the sort of conflicts humorously pictured in the little poem which appears above are permitted to go on unresolved all through life. If a man is to be a consistent, integrated personality he has got to make up his mind which shall be dominant, the purpose to "love his brother as himself" or, on the other hand, to "think of naught but power and pelf."

No one, perhaps, ever achieves a completely integrated personality. There always are and must be conflicts, tensions between the higher and the lower, between the flesh and the spirit; within the soul of man, also, there reverberate the conflicts between the standards and values of the social groups with which he is in any way identified. But the measure of his maturity is the measure of his inner integration. Utter disintegration, complete lack of consistency, is madness.

How is integration—inner unity and consistency— achieved? It is really perfectly clear and simple. Such integration is achieved by the establishment of a dominant purpose in life. When one's whole will is set upon the accomplishment of a purpose which is believed to be of all-commanding worth the scattered forces of personality rally and are unified about the drive for the accomplishment of that purpose.

Such integration, of course, may be accomplished upon very different moral levels. The ruthless, exploiting enterprisers—such as Jay Gould, John Jacob Astor, or Russell Sage—or world conquerors—such as Alexander, Napoleon or Hitler—were, I suppose, well-integrated personalities. They were consumed by one all-dominating purpose which unified the tremendous drives of their powerful personalities for the accomplishment of the ends they sought. But often the ends they sought brought enormous grief and suffering to untold millions. All of which means that it is not enough to have an integrated personality, and inner consistency and unity of purpose. The purpose to be achieved must be a worthy one if the resulting integrated personality is to be admirable.

Professor Edgar Sheffield Brightman, of Boston, used to say: "Everybody wants something. The practical man is the man who knows how to get what he wants. The philosopher is the man who knows what he ought to want. The ideal man is the man who knows how to get what he ought to want." And, perhaps one might add, who not only *knows* how to get what he ought to want but goes about getting it.

This problem of moral discrimination to which Professor Brightman calls attention is certainly one of paramount importance. It is not enough to sing, as a popular song does,

"I Want What I Want, When I Want It!" The question is: What ought one to want? What are the things most worth seeking after? What purposes are worthy to command our devotion? What values should direct our striving? To what purposes shall one give one's life in order that it may attain its true fulfilment? What great ends should command one's endeavor in order that one may become not merely an integrated personality but also a good man?

Here, of course, is where intelligence performs its function. For we men are not, like the dumb brutes, the mere servants of impulse. To us is given the capacity to think abstractly, to consider alternative courses of action, to judge values, to think critically, and deliberately to adopt chosen courses of conduct. We may weigh and consider. Truly, impulse drives strongly, but it can be held in abeyance until intelligent decision is reached.

To each man various alternatives are offered as goals for his striving. Wealth, fame and power beckon. Sensual gratification is a lure for many. But the truly wise man sees beyond immediate but transient satisfactions and seeks more lasting values. The religious man seeks goals for his endeavor which have permanent and universal validity. Where are these abiding values to be found?

It is all in the Gospel. "Seek ye first the Kingdom of God, and His righteousness," said Jesus, "and all these things—the necessary things of life—shall be added unto you." What is the *first* commandment, that is, what is the all-embracing will of God for man? "Thou shalt love the

Lord thy God, with all thy heart, with all thy soul, and with all thy mind. This is the first and great commandment. And a second is like unto it. Thou shalt love thy neighbor as thyself." And in the fulfilment of that command is our greatest freedom and our highest destiny.

This, then, must be our all-dominating purpose. The simple observable fact is that the demands which social living make upon us cannot be met by selfish indulgence. This actual world is which we live, if ever it is to be a fit place for man, requires a real sharing of life, a real control of one's purposes and activities by an attitude of loving good will. It requires love for and devotion to God, whose will is our good; and love for and service to our fellows whose life we share. Nothing less than this can serve as a dominant purpose if our lives are to achieve satisfactory integration and are to come to their full fruition. Love binds together both the inner life of the individual and the larger life of society.

No better illustration of a life completely unified by loving purpose can be found than that of the Master Himself. He envisaged a world in which men should live together in terms of mutual love and respect; a society which should be better than the kingdoms of this world, not so much because of better schemes of social organization, but because of better motives in the hearts of men. And in His own life He exemplified the virtues of the Kingdom. Love unified the tremendous energies of His majestic personality about the noblest aims and purposes, and also made Him a sharer of the lives and interests of all men in all ages, rich and poor, virtuous and sinful, happy and wretched, and a sharer, too, of the love and life and purpose of God Himself. This is personality unification at its loftiest and best. "And He has given us an example that we should follow in His steps."

CHAPTER 6

Make Habit Your Ally

My professor of psychology, many years ago, used to say that every minister ought to preach at least one sermon each year based on William James' chapter on "Habit" in his *Principles of Psychology*.[1] It is a very famous chapter, and doubtless many sermons have been based upon it. If you have not read the chapter lately, it might be profitable to read it again. It carries a message that should not only make us think more deeply but act more wisely.

A sort of digest of the whole chapter is found in James' exhortation: "Make your nervous system your ally instead of your enemy." Perhaps the best way to start is to explore and summarize what Professor James says in developing this theme.

First, he points out that, from the physiological standpoint, an acquired habit is nothing else than *a new pathway of discharge formed in the brain by which incoming currents tend to escape*. Now, that sounds a bit technical, but

[1] Quotations are from *Principles of Psychology*, pp. 112, 114, 122, 123-126, Vol. I, Chapter IV, by William James. Used by permission of the publishers, Henry Holt and Company, Inc.

it is very important. For the function of the brain and nervous system is to receive impressions from the external world through the sense organs, transmit them through the nerves to the brain or spinal cord, which in turn directs appropriate overt behavior on the part of the organism. As James says, "The currents come in and must find a way out." In the lower animals, "the way out" for these currents is pretty well determined by instinct—in insects almost completely so, but in the higher animals, such as dogs and horses, there is much room for learning and the formation of habit. Consequently, we can train animals. In man, this possibility of learning and establishment of habits is at its highest. When the current comes in as a result of an external stimulus, and finds its way out into overt behavior, it must either follow an old path—perhaps something laid down in the nervous system as an instinct or a reflex—or it may find a new path as a result of learning or thinking. But every time the current runs over such a source it cuts deeper the channel in the nervous system and makes it that much easier for the current to run that way next time. This is the physiological basis of habit; it is this that makes habit so compelling. We bind ourselves by inner chains, as it were, either to that which is desirable or to that which is undesirable. Being what we are, there is no escape from it. Whether we will or no we inevitably are "creatures of habit." Habit does indeed become "second nature." You cannot decide whether or not habit will control a large part of your behavior. You can only decide whether or not yours shall be good habits.

In the second place Professor James points out that this formation of habit has *important practical effects*. Of these he names two that are particularly notable:

"First, habit simplifies our movements, makes them accurate, and diminishes fatigue."

I am sure that this really requires no illustration if we think about it for a minute. Did you ever watch a child learning to tie its shoelaces, or to write, or even to walk? Suppose we had to go through all that every time we wanted to put on our shoes, write a letter, or walk across the room? We do these things easily—write letters, for example (or perhaps that is not a good example, considering how slow some people are to reply to my letters!)—but at any rate we do it with whatever ease we do, not because it is natural, but because it is "second nature," a learned activity which has become habit. During World War I visited a couple of the schools which were set up in the army camps for illiterates, and it made me feel very ill at ease to watch the painful efforts which some of these grown men were making with big, clumsy hands to form letters. And they were quite intelligent men; indeed, psychological tests showed some of them to be considerably above average. But they had never learned to write. The necessary channels to ease in writing never had been cut through their nervous systems, and their fingers were awkward as those of little children—indeed, probably even more so. What most of us do with ease was a physically and nervously exhausting task for these men.

A second important practical effect of habit formation is

that "habit diminishes the conscious attention with which our acts are performed." The importance of this fact can hardly be overstated. If we had to give conscious attention to the performance of every act instead of letting habit direct these acts almost unconsciously, our time and attention would be so completely taken up that we should hardly be able to live a human life. We should be much like the centipede who got along all right until he tried to remember which foot went after which, when he walked, so that he might control his locomotion more deliberately, but finally he got so mixed up that he rolled over in the ditch completely helpless. I am sure that I couldn't tell you where the letter "y" is on my typewriter, but I hit it every time I want it without hunting for it—or most times, anyway. My machine is still a bit weak on spelling. At any rate, finding those letters is now committed to my nervous system; it has become habit. I don't have to give the matter conscious attention. And I can think about what I am writing rather than about the location of the keys.

But it is the ethical importance of the principle of habit, as Professor James points out, that commands our chief attention. Habit is, he says, "the enormous fly-wheel of society," it is society's "most precious conservative agent." That is, while bad habits will bind men to evil ways, good habits—that is, the agreed-upon forms of behavior which make for social well-being and which have been so ingrained by training and habit that most people follow them automatically—keep society going in orderly fashion. It is in discussing this matter that William James says what I have indicated as a sort of text for the chapter: "The great thing, then, in all education, is to *make our nervous system our ally rather than our enemy*. It is to fund and capitalize our acquisitions, and live at ease upon the interest of the fund. For this, we must make automatic and habitual, as early as possible, as many useful actions as we can, and guard against growing into ways that are likely to be disadvantageous to us, as we should guard against the plague. The more of the details of our daily life we can hand over to the effortless custody of automatism, the more our higher powers of mind will be set free for their own proper work." For the accomplishment of this purpose he gives four maxims, two of which he has borrowed from Professor Bain.

The first maxim is: In the acquisition of a new habit, or the leaving off of an old one, we must take care to *launch ourselves with as strong and decided an initiative as possible.*

The second maxim is: *Never suffer an exception to occur until the new habit is securely rooted in your life.*

The third maxim is: *Seize the very first possible opportunity to act on every resolution you make, and on every emotional prompting you may experience in the direction of the habits you aspire to gain.*

And fourth: *Keep the faculty of effort alive in you by a little gratuitous effort every day.*

It may seem presumptuous to add even a footnote to what Professor James has to say about habit, but I should like to suggest some implications of what we know about habit for the cultivation of the moral and religious life.

And the first of these implications is that *the formation of habit may involve either slavery or freedom.*

On the one hand, if our choices are wrong, and we become habituated in evil, we find ourselves with inner chains to the evil thing. "Sin," said Jeremy Taylor, "startles a man, that is the first step; then it becomes pleasing, then easy, then delightful, then frequent and habitual; then the man is importunate, then obstinate, then resolves never to repent, and then is damned." There is a verse of Scripture that says it, "His own sin shall take the wicked himself, and he shall be holden with the cords of his sin." No doubt you have seen pictures of that famous sculpture of Bacchus, the god of drink and revelry. He is riding a panther at a furious bound. How suggestive and true! A man may begin a career of vice and think that he has mounted a well-broken steed, that he has a firm hold on the reins and that he can stop whenever he will. But too late he finds that he is astride a savage beast that no human power can control. "The first and best victory," said Plato, "is for a man to conquer himself, and without that the conqueror is naught but the veriest slave." It was out of this consciousness of the tightening bonds of evil habit, of which the poet was sadly aware that he was unable to free himself, that Burns wrote on a sick-bed from which he feared that he would not rise again to health:

> Fain would I say, "Forgive my foul offense!"
> Fain promise never more to disobey;

But, should my Author health again dispense,
Again I might desert fair virtue's way;
Again in folly's path might go astray;
Again exalt the brute and sink the man;
Then how can I for Heavenly mercy pray,
Who act so counter Heavenly mercy's plan?
Who sin so oft have mourn'd, yet to temptation ran?

It is not so much that sins are punished, as they are in a court of justice, but that our sins punish us. Someone has said, "We are punished by our sins, not for them." The trouble is that, launched on a course of evil, we bind ourselves to the evil thing and all its evil consequences. "The gods are just, and of our pleasant vices make instruments to scourge us." It was a true insight of Milton's when he pictured Satan as flying through space and crying, "Which way I fly is hell! Myself am hell!"

Thus the building of habit, which proceeds inevitably, if one's choices are evil, means the binding of oneself in the chains of slavery.

On the other hand, however, this same process of habit formation, if one's choices are good, means liberation. One who has made good choice a habit is not troubled about making conscious moral decisions on every small matter—such choice has become as automatic for him as has evil choice for the sinner. He is set free for progress in higher realms of aspiration and achievement.

Recently I ran across a short article headed "Don't Decide to Go to Church!" and I said to myself "Here's something I must look into." But I soon found that the author was not saying, "Decide not to go to church!" What he was saying was that some people place an unnecessary burden upon themselves every Sunday morning by deciding whether or not they shall attend a worship service that day. They do not decide three times each day, he pointed out, whether or not they shall eat—the need of the body for food is taken for granted, and the decision to eat the meal is taken automatically by habit. The need for spiritual food, the author said, is equally urgent, and the decision to satisfy that need should be as automatic and habitual as is the decision to satisfy the needs of the physical organism by eating.

If that decision has been taken, and church-going has become established habit, then one is set free to get the highest values out of this one hour set apart each week for the worship of God. Each week the worshipper will be reminded that his brief life is set in eternity, and the temporal and changing things of life will take their proper places; disappointments and defeats will lose their sting as faith in the good purpose of God is renewed; injustice and wrong, so often temporarily triumphant, will be endurable in view of the assured triumph of righteousness; and all our selfishness, envy and littleness will be driven out by a contemplation of the love of God shining in the face of Jesus Christ.

The important thing to keep in mind is that it is just as easy to establish good habits as it is bad habits. But the establishment of bad habits means binding oneself in the bonds of a bitter slavery; while establishing good habits sets one free from moral struggle on low levels to ever higher aspiration and achievement.

The second implication of what we know about the psychology of habit formation is that *it is through the establishment of habit-systems that character is achieved.* And this is true whether the habit-systems are good or bad. Bad character is simply a well established system of bad habits; good character is, likewise, simply a well established system of good habits.

Many years ago I first heard the precept: "Sow a thought and reap an act; sow an act and reap a habit; sow a habit and reap a character; sow a character and reap a destiny."

And good character is surely the highest of all our human values. In 1882, Spurgeon, the great London preacher, wrote to William E. Gladstone: "You do not know how those of us regard you who feel it a joy to live when a Prime Minister believes in righteousness. We believe in no man's infallibility, but it is restful to be sure of one man's integrity." And what lay back of Gladstone's integrity of character is revealed in his intimate family life. Gladstone inculcated in his son the duty of regularity in morning and evening prayer and in daily reading of the Bible. He wrote to him, "Place habit on the side of religion. You cannot depend upon your tastes and feelings toward divine things to be uniform." He saw clearly that the foundation of good character rested upon the firm establishment of good habits.

A third implication, for morals and religion, of what we know about habit formation, is that, in order to establish a habit *one must act—not merely wish—and act, and act again*. It is the repetition of acts that cuts those channels in the nervous system through which flow the currents which direct behavior.

I think it is Huxley who tells the story of the practical joker who, seeing a discharged veteran carrying home his dinner, suddenly called out, "Attention!" whereupon the man instantly brought his hands down, and lost his mutton and potatoes in the gutter. Habit takes a tremendous hold. I notice that I almost never change my clothes during the day but that, on taking out my watch and placing it on the dresser, I start to wind it up. The habit is so firmly established from doing that every night on going to bed that I do it automatically whenever I undress. An absent-minded friend of mine in college, who started to change his clothes in the evening to go out to dinner, automatically finished the process of undressing, put on his pajamas and went to bed. He didn't realize until next morning that he had missed his dinner engagement!

The emphasis, then, must be upon *doing*. That is the point of the text, "Be ye *doers* of the word, and not *hearers* only." The great danger is that wish-thinking, daydreaming and sentimentality will substitute playing with ideas for getting to work. There are many people who would like to do great things, be important persons, achieve distinction in one line or another, but are unwilling to pay the price of hard, persistent labor. Do you remember the story of the Curies? Perhaps you saw the motion picture which told the story of their discovery of radium. Who wouldn't like, with a flash of insight, to make such a discovery? But back of that discovery lay long, disheartening, but undiscouragable labor, day after day and even year after year. The story of those who not merely dreamed, but made dreams come true, might be repeated ten thousand times. They are stories of men and women who made unremitting toil a habit, and their labors were ultimately rewarded. It is not enough to cherish an ideal or to nurse a hope—that ideal must be put to work, the dream must become a purpose for the realization of which we struggle. The latecomer at church, arriving just before the benediction, asked the usher, "Is the sermon done yet?" "No," replied the usher, "it isn't done. It's only preached."

There is something else to bear in mind, and that is that an emotion not expressed in action operates as a poison in the mental life with deadly effect upon character. There is the story of the Cuban millionaire to whom a beggar managed to gain access in spite of the defences he had built about himself. The beggar told such a tale of woe that the millionaire was melted to tears. Finally he could stand it no longer, so, calling in a member of his bodyguard, he said, "Eduardo, throw this poor devil out. He's breaking my heart!" It is precisely this sort of failure to permit an emotion to take its normal route of discharge—in a deed of practical helpfulness it would be in this case—that hinders future resolutions from receiving proper expression and so leads to the disintegration of character. It is not in the stirring of emotion that habit is formed, but it is when these emotions produce appropriate motor effects that the initiation of habit appears. If we fail in this respect, the emotions operate in the soul as does toxin in the body, and character suffers. And yet this happens so often. We feel deeply moved by a portrayal on the screen, or maybe by something we learn about children in an orphanage or other institution, or even by a sermon, but we do nothing about it. In that case we are worse off than if we had never learned anything about it. And I doubt if even giving money is enough, unless with the money we give some of ourselves. You will remember what the Master said in *The Vision of Sir Launfal*:

> Not what we give, but what we share,
> For the gift without the giver is bare;
> Who gives himself with his alms feeds three,
> Himself, his hungering neighbor, and me.

So, if you would develop good habits and build a strong and admirable character, the precepts are those which William James and others have given, and which we repeat:

Launch out in the direction you would go with a strong and decided initiative.

Never suffer an exception to occur.

Seize the very first opportunity to *act* on the resolution you have made and on every emotional prompting you may experience in the direction you aspire to go.

And, finally, keep the faculty of effort alive by a little gratuitous effort every day.

CHAPTER 7

"I Should Worry!"

WE ALL KNOW the meaning of the slang
phrase of a few years ago, "I should worry!" It means precisely, "It doesn't worry me! I don't care!" It is not that light
and flippant attitude that Jesus advised when he said: "Do
not worry about life." [1] There are times when the Christian
must care, when he ought to feel deep concern.

A rhyme written back in the days when this slang phrase
was current represents two attitudes toward worry and its
causes, both of which are dangerous.

> "I should worry! I should care!
> I should marry a millionaire.
> He should worry! He should die!
> And I should marry a regular guy."

The first, "I should worry! I should care!" represents a
flippant and irresponsible attitude which does not care what
damage may result from one's behavior; the second, "He
should worry! He should die!" represents such a continual
carrying of a burden of anxiety that the unrelieved strain
may well result in sickness and even death.

[1] Matthew 6:25 (Goodspeed translation).

Most worries, however, have deeper causes than those indicated in this verse—or, on the other hand, purely imaginary causes. In any case, "worry," as Jesus uses the term, is not an effective way of dealing with the causes of worry. Fretful, anxious care is debilitating and depressing, rendering us unable to deal intelligently and effectively with those situations which cause us anxiety. The things that Jesus talks about, for example, the affairs of daily life, food, clothing, the events of the morrow, should concern us. We should plan to provide for the meeting of these needs. But if we think about them with corroding anxiety, with fear and with dread, we not only unnecessarily increase almost unbearably the emotional load we carry, but we render ourselves ineffective even in dealing with these circumstances as they arise.

But there are multitudes of such needless worriers. Dale Carnegie has recently written a book entitled *How to Stop Worrying and Start Living*, which his publishers expect to exceed in sales the 3,500,000 copies of his best-seller, *How to Win Friends and Influence People*. I do not know whether or not they are over-optimistic as to sales but, if they are not, then there are a lot of people over-pessimistic as to life. If Dale Carnegie can help reduce the number of worriers he will have done mankind a service, while at the same time he will have reduced his causes for worry about his own financial future. Unless he starts to worry about the possibility of all the banks going broke. After all, you can always find something to worry about if you want to.

Many of our worst worriers are victims of too vivid imaginations. They imagine threats and menaces that are not there at all, or they build up a remote possibility into an immediately impending disaster. There is the story of the lady who made it a practice when arriving at a strange hotel to make sure exactly where the fire escapes were. Exploring around the floor on which her room was located, she looked into a bath-room and found it occupied by an elderly gentleman. "Oh, I beg your pardon," she said. "I was looking for the fire escape!" and hurried away. In a moment she heard the pad of feet behind her, and a shout made her turn. "Hey!" gasped the old gentleman, who was clad only in a bath towel, "where's the fire?" Thus we often build up alarms on very slight occasion. Many of our worries have as little real cause as that.

Leroy Phelps, who filmed Frank Buck's "Bring 'Em Back Alive" and other travel and exploration films, was in Guatemala not long ago making a picture depicting life in this country. While here he told me about something he saw in the Belgian Congo. The fishermen in a certain lake have a unique fishing technique. There is a time each day when the sun shines directly overhead, and the fishermen go out with a long line tied between two boats. To this line, at brief intervals, are attached wooden floats. The sun, shining overhead on the clear waters of this lake, sends shadows of these floats right to the bottom of the lake, and the fish-eye view, apparently, is that a series of bars run from the lake surface to the bottom. Gradually the fishermen tow the floats to shore, with the fish being driven before these insubstantial bars, until they come to the shallow water where men stand and throw the fish ashore. One quickly sees the moral. At any time the fish could have swum through these shadow bars and been free, but the imagined bars imprisoned them and they were captured through their fears. There is no more substance than that to many of the things that cause us anxiety and make us prisoners to our fears. We allow ourselves to suffer from fears that have no substance of reality.

It is precisely this sort of thing, I think, that Jesus is talking about in his Sermon on the Mount. "Do not worry about life, wondering what you will have to eat, or to drink, or about your body, wondering what you will have to wear. Is not life more important than food, and the body than clothes? Look at the wild birds . . . Your heavenly Father feeds them. Are you not of more account than they? . . . See how the wild flowers grow . . . If God so beautifully dresses the wild grass . . . will he not much more surely clothe you?"

This is not, I am sure, to be interpreted as an encouragement to lack of thrift and foresight. Elsewhere, you will remember, Jesus advises men first to count the cost before they begin to build a house. What he is cautioning against is that nagging worry about the ordinary needs of life which wear so many people out, and he advises men, on the other hand, to have faith in the good providence of God who will sustain our efforts and provide for our needs. We are to do the best we can and then rest confident in the good purposes of God.

I read the other day about a business man who was a chronic worrier, and determined to find out just how much grounds he had for worrying. On analysing his situation he found that 40 per cent of his worries were about things that were never likely to happen; 30 per cent were about past decisions that could not be changed; 12 per cent concerned others' criticisms of himself that didn't matter anyway; 10 per cent dealt with his health which he was already doing his best to protect. Only 8 per cent, he decided, were legitimate causes of worry. If we could reduce our worries, as this man did, by 92 per cent, we should be getting somewhere. If men generally did this, we could add enormously to the total sum of human happiness and effectiveness.

There is another kind of worry, however, which is really serious, and which usually is a consequence of psychological conditioning in childhood. Such a worrier is harassed, strained, tense, and yet is unable to put his finger on the cause of his worries—in fact, everything worries him, life worries him, he worries himself. Of course the psychologists have found a name for this condition. Such a person suffers from "anxiety-neurosis."

What causes this condition? It is not the ordinary problems of everyday life that worry him, although the slightest difficulties may upset him terribly. The real causes lie deeper. They root back in the relations of the child with his parents, nurses, or others in authority, in the impressionable days of early childhood. Many people are handicapped all their lives because of the influence upon them as little children of hide-bound, fear-inspiring, guilt-inducing parents. The child who grows up in a home where he is loved and trusted, where strong and self-reliant parents so guide him that he moves out into life with confidence, where the whole atmosphere of the home breathes faith in God and trust in the goodness of life, will grow up free of such basic anxieties. But where the parents lack real love for the child, where they themselves are strained and fearful, where unreasoning prohibitions are enforced by threats and the inducing of feelings of guilt and fear, a profound anxiety comes to possess the child in his relations with his parents, which in time comes to characterize his relationships with all his fellows, and with the universe itself.

The only really effective way to deal with this problem is to provide homes for our children in which they will grow up feeling loved and secure. Homes in which there is real affection between husband and wife and between parents and children, where common sense prevails, and where there is confidence in the goodness of life, based on a vital faith in God, are the ones which will produce children with healthy mental initiative and well-balanced emotions.

For those who, unfortunately, find themselves in mature life suffering these basic anxieties, there still is hope, if they can be helped to understand the circumstances out of which their unfortunate condition arose, and if they will resolutely undertake to reconstruct both their thinking and their action. But this task of re-educating the emotions is likely to be a long and difficult one, and will require great courage and determination.

Sometimes these anxieties are almost miraculously cleared away by a complete commitment to and an unquestioning faith in the goodness of God. Prayer is often the instrument through which this transformation is effected. My friend, Dr. William S. Sadler of Chicago, an eminent psychiatrist and author of more than a dozen important books, tells in his monumental *Theory and Practice of Psychiatry* [2] about such a case. He and his wife, Dr. Lena K. Sadler, now unfortunately deceased, practiced together, she as a general physician, he as a psychiatrist. On one occasion Dr. Lena sent to him a young woman suffering from general anxiety and severely depressed. "How long will it take to cure her?" Dr. Lena asked. "Oh, about a year," he answered, briefly describing the various steps that would have to be accomplished before cure could be expected. Dr. Lena said nothing, but not long after Dr. Sadler saw the patient who seemed both well and happy. Stumped, he asked the patient what had happened. "Oh," she replied, "Dr. Lena taught me how to pray!" None of the steps that he had prescribed had been by-passed—straightening up wrong relationships, righting past mistakes, redirecting the emotions. But prayer had speeded up the time required for their accomplishment. It still is true, as Tennyson said:

> More things are wrought by prayer
> Than this world dreams of.

But, in the kind of chancy world in which we live, there

[2] By permission of Funk & Wagnalls Company, publishers.

are plenty of real causes for worry—or at least for anxiety and deep concern. There are sickness, accident, sudden death, financial disaster, family difficulties. And, today, there hangs over the world the menace of war with its unforeseeable possibilities of disaster and doom. Yes, in such a world as ours there is plenty to worry about.

And what shall we say to all this? Well, there are two things to say:

First, many of the situations which cause us anxiety can be improved, if intelligently faced; and many of the causes of worry can be completely removed.

During the war I saw a letter from a young lieutenant in the Canadian army, written to his father who was terribly anxious and depressed. All his children were in the army, and his business was threatened with disaster. Said the young lieutenant, "Remember, dad, the old saying, 'The difficulties of life decrease the moment they are faced!'" And that is true. We can often do something to relieve the difficulty if we will face it; we are lost if we will not.

This applies to our personal problems. In a recent Chicago paper appeared the story of a young Chicago woman, a victim of cerebral palsy of a type which causes a constant, involuntary motion of the muscles, who faced and overcame her handicap. I knew another Chicago woman, a victim of this disease, who completely retreated from life and suffered immeasurable misery. Such persons suffer not only the handicap of their illness, but must face the reluctance of society to accept them as eligible for normal activities. Said this young woman, "The day I accepted my handicap,

I began to relax." She recalls that she started to walk at eight, learning by pushing a buggy and riding a tricycle. She read aloud to herself to master speech. She was undiscouraged by the pity other students had for her. Now, at twenty-six, she can point to a long list of academic and clinical attainments, including a Master's degree at the University of Chicago, where she did extensive research. Her very handicap has, indeed, opened a road to important service to others. She has lectured and counselled both parents and children extensively. She was clinical psychologist last year for a crippled children's home in Jamestown, N. Y. At the time the article appeared she was giving a four-week lecture course to parents and other interested persons at the Chicago Psychological Institute. Her word to parents is: "Remember your handicapped child as an individual, not as an abnormal physical body." And her word to the handicapped child is: "Accept your limitation. The world owes you nothing. You owe it as much as does the non-handicapped."

The principle applies with regard to large social problems just as truly as to personal problems. Take this most serious and menacing problem of our time, the problem of war. Surely we have not reached a place where we are willing to abdicate our intelligence and resort to force and violence, with all their devastating consequences, as the means of resolving our basic social conflicts. As Raymond L. Fosdick, President of the Rockefeller Foundation, has said:

"Force seems to be such an easy answer. It appears to cut

through the complexity and confusion without the necessity of the severe intellectual effort and discipline involved in creating any effective alternative."

There is our problem, and the tragedy is that so many people, who have no faith in force as a means of solving these problems but who see clearly enough that it only leaves the problem more complicated, yet surrender to it when there seems nothing else to do. If what former Secretary of State James F. Byrnes said is true, "Today the world must take its choice. There must be one world for all of us or there will be no world for any of us," then we must find some alternative to force. We must make the United Nations work, of course. But something deeper than that is required. In this economically interdependent world, we must be educated into a common social consciousness. We must extend the consciousness of community beyond national boundaries to include the whole world. We must affirm this world-wide network of human relationships as compelling a world-wide social consciousness. And, in that frame of mind, we must insist upon the persistent application of intelligence to the solution of the problems that now menace our hopes and dreams.

But, second, there still remain some things that cause anxiety and distress which cannot be changed or removed— the incurable cancer, the permanent injury, the inevitable death which we all face. Sometimes it seems that, do what we may, life is faced by ultimate frustration and defeat, and that all our efforts are vain.

The only answer is the answer of faith. Our Christian

religion is the one of all the world's great faiths which most realistically faces the problems of death, disaster and apparent defeat. Our Lord is not one who, after many struggles, won out over his enemies and "lived happily ever afterward." He died in agony and shame, a victim of his enemies, on a cross. But that death is seen to have redemptive quality; and that disaster is seen, in the light of the centuries, to have been the world's greatest triumph.

In many and mysterious ways, and with our cooperation, the loving God is working out a great purpose of good for His human children. We may trust Him. And we may work with Him. And when worse comes to worst we shall find mysteriously provided strength and courage to face whatever must be faced. The God who did not fail Christ, and into whose hands at the last He was able to commend His spirit, will not fail us.

The sovereign cure for worry, then, of every kind, is Christian faith. The Bible has the answer to our need: "Fret not thyself. . . . Trust in the Lord. . . . Commit thy way unto Him and He shall bring it to pass."

A minister has suggested that in all our churches we should have a second collection—but not for money. He proposes that, at the conclusion of the service, just before the benediction, huge baskets should be passed, and into these all the people should dump their cares and worries. Then, when the baskets were brought forward, the minister, acting in the name of God, would say: "I hereby declare that you are freed from your fears. Go in peace, and may the peace of God go with you."

CHAPTER 8

Your Ups and Downs

IT WAS THE beloved Robert Louis Stevenson who said: "There is no duty we so much underrate as the duty of happiness." We all want to be happy, yet few of us are thoroughly happy. "Most men," Thoreau said, "live lives of quiet desperation." Possibly we might find happiness if we could say with the Apostle, "I have learned in whatsoever state I am therewith to be content," but that is hard to say.

The fact is that, like the elevator operator, we all have our ups and downs. "Sometimes I'm up, sometimes I'm down," the Negro slave used to sing in one of his spirituals. And we all share that experience. Sometimes we are very much up, and sometimes very much down. The "up" phase we can stand, but the "down" phase is often hard to take, particularly when it continues over a long period. But life is made up of such alternations of mood. At one time we may say with Robert Browning:

How good is man's life, the mere living, how fit to employ
All the heart and the soul and the senses forever in joy!

88

But presently we may say with the exhausted and disheartened Elijah, as he lay under the juniper tree:

"It is enough; now, O Lord, take away my life."

Harry A. Overstreet in his book *About Ourselves* [1] has given names to these alternating mood-swings—they are the *micro-manic* and the *micro-depressive* moods. That is to say, they are cut from the same emotional cloth as the manic-depressive psychosis and, if allowed to go to a sufficient extreme, will eventuate in that unfortunate mental disorder. We need to guard our moods and seek a balanced emotional life. We need to take seriously our "duty of happiness."

Few people, I think, would want to live continually in what Dr. Overstreet calls the micro-manic phase—the sense of restless energy, high excitability, frothy cheerfulness and unreasonable exaltation. Perhaps you have heard of the man who abandoned a religious cult to which he had been enthusiastically attached and, when asked why he had left it, replied: "O, I got tired of being so confoundedly happy!" We need some changes of mood. Dr. Conrad Sommer, former medical director of the Illinois Society for Mental Hygiene, has expressed the opinion that people who experience changes of mood are better able to sympathise with others on their "off" days, and to be more tolerant of the actions of the over-elated on the "on" days, than persons of a too even temperament. Moreover, he thinks, they are better able to appreciate the fine arts, par-

[1] Published by W. W. Norton & Co., Inc.

ticularly the range of moods found in poetry, music, paint-
ing and the drama. A person who never feels the "blues" is
likely to have little patience with that large number of people over whose lives a dark shadow often rests.

Let us look at this matter of the "blues" for a little while,
for it is a very serious problem. Great unhappiness is something to be avoided, if at all possible, for, while many unhappy people have contributed enormously to the enrich-
ment of our common life, others have failed miserably on
account of it. Life has been for them a major disaster. Happiness in itself is one of our greatest human
goods.

There are people who suffer depression with adequate
reason, as far as the external circumstances of life are concerned; there are others whose sufferings seem to have no
adequate cause, and who are depressed either because of
hidden conflicts, physical disorders, or as a result of
constitutional factors which are hard to discover and
treat.

The persons most easy to help are those whose depressions have readily discoverable causes. During the war I
had the privilege of doing a good deal of work with the
U.S.O. Clubs, and the Director of one of these U.S.O.'s
told me about a soldier who visited his Club. He saw the
soldier sitting morosely apart from the crowd. The Director
felt that something was wrong, and sat down beside him.
He found him dreadfully depressed, and at first unwilling
to talk. Finally the soldier said, "Mr. W. . . . I haven't a

damn thing to live for. When I get up the nerve I'm going to kill myself."

The Director hid the shock he felt as well as he could, and said, "Let's go back in my office where we'll be alone, and talk about it. There may be some way out."

He learned that the soldier, before the war, had been the owner of a small but growing business in an Iowa town. He had worked long hours, made equipment, built additions to the original structure, and spent considerable money in redecorating. He had a wife and two fine children. When the war came he volunteered, feeling that he would be drafted anyway. He was sent overseas and saw a good deal of combat. In December, 1943, his home and plant were burned to the ground, snuffing out the lives of his wife and children. He received this tragic news while he was himself in the hospital recuperating from wounds received in action.

The soldier did not find it easy to talk. At first he spoke with great difficulty, but, finding a willing listener, went on to unburden himself of the load of pain, grief and loneliness which, up until now, he had been carrying alone. That in itself seemed to give him considerable relief. When discharged from the hospital he had started back home, but now, almost on the threshold, seemed unable to go farther and face the scene of his former happiness. Why should he go on living, when everything that made life worth while was gone? The Director did not try to persuade him against suicide, but soon led him to discuss other possible ways of meeting the problem. Now, with the emotional strain somewhat relieved, he seemed glad to explore the possibilities. They did not arrive at any definite and final plan, but the soldier said that he would have to think more about it. He did, however, say that he would go back home and then make up his mind what to do. They then went together to the Director's home for supper and, while at the supper, the soldier asked the Director, who was a Salvation Army officer, if he would remember him in his prayers. They had a brief prayer at the table, and the Director promised that he would keep him in his prayers during the difficult days ahead.

About a month later the Director received a letter from the soldier, thanking him for what he had done. He said that friends had been kind, and that he was now working and was going to start all over again.

Unfortunately all cases do not turn out so happily. As Dr. Karl A. Menninger says, "All depressed people are potential suicides."[2] The first military funeral which it was my duty to conduct in World War II was that of a chum of my son's, a sensitive lad who had published distinguished poetry, but who found life in the army, with its necessary regimentation and stifling of individuality so intolerable that, in a fit of depression, he took his own life. Eleanor Stevenson, a Red Cross worker overseas during the war, told in an article in the *Saturday Evening Post* in October 1944, of a young soldier in Italy, who had gone through a

[2] From *The Human Mind*, by Karl A. Menninger. By permission of the publishers, Alfred A. Knopf, Inc.

great deal of combat and whose outfit was under orders to return to the front lines, coming to talk to one of the Red Cross girls. He was evidently under great tension. "I've taken all I can," he said. "I'm through. I can't go back there again. I'll shoot myself first!" The girl thought it best not to take the threat seriously, and passed it off lightly. "Why not go out and shoot a few Germans first?" she asked. The young soldier went back to his tent and an hour later was found dead. He had put a bullet through his head.

Probably it is the most sensitive persons, those most keenly aware of the tragic aspects of life, and therefore most likely to get under the burden of human sorrow and help relieve it, who are most liable to depression. Abraham Lincoln was such a one. It has been often surmised that his melancholy was partly caused by organic disorders—malfunctioning of the liver or gastro-intestinal system. But, if there were such disorders, it is quite as likely that they were caused by emotional disturbance as that they were the causes of his dark moods. Constitutionally he was of a melancholy temperament. He was incapacitated for months after the death of Ann Rutledge. At a later date, during a long period of depression, he was kept in guarded seclusion, and all knives or other instruments with which he might injure himself were removed from his reach. On the day set for his wedding to Mary Todd the guests assembled, but Lincoln did not appear. He was found in his room in a state of deepest dejection, overwhelmed by feelings of unworthiness and hopelessness. He was, he said, the most miserable man living. "If what I feel were equally distributed to the whole human family, there would not be one cheerful face on earth. Whether I shall ever be better, I cannot tell; I awfully forebode I shall not." This was the man who carried on his heart the burden of millions of black men living in bondage, and, indeed, the bitterness, folly and pain of the distressed everywhere, the man whose "tender, tragic, ever-changing face," even as pictured in bronze in the great Lincoln Memorial in Washington, moves all observers deeply. Perhaps it is only the man who is capable of deep personal sorrow who can share the tragic load of other people's grief.

There is no evidence, of course, that Jesus suffered anything like melancholia, but a careful reading of the stories of the temptation in the wilderness and of the agony in the garden of Gethsemane will persuade us that Jesus knew severe depression of spirits. "Could ye not pray with me one hour?" He asked his disciples who had fallen asleep while, in such torment that "He sweat, as it were, great drops of blood," He prayed the Father, "If it be possible, let this cup pass from Me." "We have not an High Priest who cannot be touched with a feeling of our infirmities," says the author of the Letter to the Hebrews.

But neither Jesus nor Lincoln lived permanently under a cloud. They were both, indeed, "made perfect through suffering." But they came out from the darkness and lived with calm confidence in the abiding good purpose of God. And that good purpose they sought to fulfil in their own lives. Indeed, Jesus could speak of a peace which remained through all the stormy circumstances of life with those who would abide in God's will. This was the peace He would bestow upon His followers. He even went farther. "These things I have spoken unto you," He said, "that My joy might remain in you, and that your joy might be full!" "Blessed [that is, happy] are they that mourn, for they shall be comforted." It is inevitable in this life that men shall suffer, and there are few who will escape some dark hours of grave depression. But it is the purpose of God that we shall find peace, and even more than peace—happiness and joy.

How are we to accomplish our "duty of happiness?" How can we overcome these dark hours of depression, and learn with the Apostle "in whatsoever state we are, therewith to be content"? I wish I knew an easy and certain answer. If anyone could say with confidence, "Do these things; 1-2-3, and all will be well," he could make a fortune. Probably there is no such panacea, but there are some tested ways of reaching a happier frame of mind, and, perhaps, if we will resolutely work at them, we may be helped.

One thing we have learned, and that is that there is little profit in telling the depressed person to "cheer up!" That is exactly what he can't do, and it only annoys and irritates him to be confronted with this superficial cheeriness. But the individual can, if he has sufficient resolution, take himself in hand and force a smile even he doesn't feel like it. And it is remarkable what keeping the corners of your mouth turned up will do after a while. Smile, and presently someone will smile back at you, just as, if you look glumly at others, they will look back unhappily at you. There is a poem of James Whitcomb Riley's which always has had a cheering effect upon me:

> O heart of mine, we shouldn't
> > Worry so!
> What we've missed of calm, we couldn't
> > Have, you know!
> What we've met of stormy pain,
> And of sorrow's driving rain,
> We can better meet again
> > If it blow.
>
> We have erred in that dark hour
> > We have known,
> When the tears fell with the shower,
> > All alone——
> Were not shine and shower blent
> As the gracious Master meant?
> Let us temper our content
> > With His own.
>
> For we know, not every morrow
> > Can be sad;
> So, forgetting all the sorrow
> > We have had,
> Let us fold away our fears,
> And put by our foolish tears,
> And through all the coming years,
> > Just be glad! [3]

Well, some will say, that is all very well for those who can do it, but this thing goes too deep with me. I can't shake it off, or talk myself out of it. And that is literally

[3] "Kissing the Rod," by James Whitcomb Riley, from *Pipes o' Pan at Zekesbury*. Used by permission of Bobbs Merrill Company, Inc.

true of many. When there is frequent and persistent depression, when it seems that the clouds will never break and that there is nothing to live for, something is seriously wrong. The trouble is not then with external circumstances, although the individual will lay hold on any untoward happening and magnify it; the real trouble is within. The first thing to do in such a case is to have a thorough physical examination and, if required, proper treatment. The trouble may lie in some glandular or organic dysfunction. If that fails, probably psychiatric treatment is indicated. And yet psychiatrists themselves confess that they stand almost helpless before depression. Their best treatment is rest, relief from strain, the opportunity given the patient to talk over his troubles, and constant protection so that the patient will not injure himself. The encouragement they give is that this is the most highly recoverable of all mental disorders. The patient will practically always recover if he does not destroy himself while in the depths of his slump. The suffering individual can help himself, too, if, even in the darkest hour, he can say, "This, too, will pass." But those who have charge of gravely depressed persons should always remember that they stand in danger. At a Seminar for Counselors which I once conducted, an army hospital worker told about a crippled soldier who had threatened suicide. "But I didn't pay any attention," she said. "He was only seeking sympathy." An army psychiatrist who was present, however, was on his feet at once, and said, "Don't ever take a chance like that! You never can tell. If any patient in my hospital even hints that he is not sure that life is worth living, I have him watched constantly. Not only are depressed persons potential suicides, but they are devilishly ingenious in finding ways to accomplish their purpose."

But most depressions are not as serious as that. We feel blue and "down," but we know we'll feel better tomorrow, or the day after anyway. Perhaps next week we'll be on top of the world. But we wish we could keep out of such emotional tail-spins. Such moods are, in considerable measure, under our control. Here are a few rules:

First: Tell your troubles to somebody you trust and who, you feel, will try to understand. Even though you can't tell why you feel blue, just talk about it. A burden shared is a burden lightened. Such emotional catharsis, as the psychiatrists call it, will almost always bring relief. As one lives with an emotional problem alone it grows and grows until the burden becomes unbearable. Just talking it out will help.

Second: Try to get a realistic view of what causes your depression. Perhaps you can rid yourself of it; perhaps you will have to learn to carry it. There are limits to what intelligence can do in controlling emotional problems, but it can do something. Perhaps it can help get rid of some of the excess emotional load. "We must not exceed our limited weight budget," Anne Lindbergh tells us, in her *North to the Orient*. And she tells of the careful sorting and re-sorting of the articles they would carry on the trip until they got down to absolute essentials. If we would do the same kind of sorting of our mental baggage and rid ourselves of non-essentials, we might free ourselves of many causes of depression. If the cause of the depression is something that can't be removed we must learn to live with it. Others have. Paul prayed that the thorn might be removed from his flesh, but it wasn't. He did learn to say, however, "Thy grace is sufficient for me."

Third: Try to think less of yourself, and more of others. Self-centeredness and self-pity are perhaps the greatest enemies of our happiness. "John," said the young wife to her husband as, with their two small children, they stood watching the lions at the Zoo, "if the lions should break out, whom would you save first, me or the children?" And without a moment's hesitation the husband replied, "Me!" Well, there is a lot of "Me first!" in the world, and it brings little happiness even to those who are seeking thus to please themselves. What we need more than anything else in order to find real happiness is to be rid of our self-centeredness and self-pity, out of which so much of our depression arises. We need to lose ourselves in the lives of other persons, to become happily participating members of a social group committed to higher ends than mere self-gratification. It is in thus losing ourselves, as seeking merely narrow, individual satisfactions, that we find ourselves on higher and happier levels of social living.

Fourth: Find a cause to which you can commit yourself, so great and commanding that your petty concerns are dwarfed into insignificance. It is thus that life's meaning is found, for we are made for higher ends than mere self-gratification. Hitler and Mussolini gained their following by calling men to something greater than the pursuit of narrow self-interest. They asked men to serve a cause in which they might discover a meaning for their lives by sharing in the fulfilment of a national ambition. The evil lay in the fact that the cause was too narrow—nationalistic domination—and the means of achieving it unethical. But the appeal lay in the fact that the goal sought was larger-than-self; it gave direction and meaning to effort and swamped the pettiness of mere individualism. The only adequate goal that has ever been offered for human striving, in which petty concerns might be lost and life's true meaning found, is that of the Kingdom of God—God's will dominant in the life of the individual, of the world and of all creation. The man who finds something to do that will count in advancing that Kingdom has gone a long way toward escape from the miasma of depression. He lives in a different climate.

Fifth: Have faith in God. Belief in God matters. What Communists believe evidently matters—they will impose their faith on the world if they can; they will die for their faith if necessary. A missionary friend has told me about watching Chinese Communists led to execution, with heads held high and unafraid. The ultimate victory, they were sure, was with them. If, when a man says he believes in God, he means, "I suppose that there is some kind of Divine Being," that doesn't matter much. He might as well believe the opposite. But if he means that he commits his life to God, that he trusts God to bring his life to its proper fulfilment, that he will do God's will though the heavens fall, that matters tremendously.

I like the man who faces what he must
With step triumphant and a heart of cheer;
Who fights the daily battle without fear;

Sees his hopes fail, yet keeps unfaltering trust
That God is God—that somehow, true and just
His plans work out for mortals.

There are too many people carrying unnecessary burdens that cause them anxiety and depression. An old lady, carrying a heavy grip, just managed to catch a train before it moved out of the station. Standing in the aisle, she still held her grip, until the conductor noticing, said, "You can put it down now, lady. The train will carry it for you!" We carry unnecessary loads. "Cast thy burden on the Lord, for He careth for thee."

There is no resource available to help people overcome grave depression equal to unfaltering faith in God. Dr. J. A. Hadfield, one of the greatest living psychotherapists, is quoted as saying in a public lecture:

Speaking as a student of psychotherapy, who, as such, has no concern with theology, I am convinced that the Christian religion is one of the most valuable and potent influences that we possess for producing that harmony and peace of mind and that confidence of soul which is needed to bring health and power to a large number of nervous patients. . . . I have attempted to cure nervous patients with suggestions of quietness and confidence, but without success until I have linked these suggestions on to that faith in the power of God which is the substance of the Christian's confidence and hope. Then the patient has become strong.[4]

[4] From *Psychology and Morals*, by J. A. Hadfield, by permission of the publishers, Robert M. McBride & Company.

The Psalmist undoubtedly knew what depression was when he said: "Out of the depths have I cried unto Thee, O Lord. Lord, hear my voice!" But it was a happier hour when he said, "I waited patiently for the Lord; and He inclined unto me and heard my voice. He brought me up also out of an horrible pit, out of the miry clay, and set my foot upon a rock, and established my goings. And He hath put a new song in my mouth, even praise unto our God."

Faith in God is the sovereign cure for depression. He will save when all else fails.

CHAPTER 9

That Inferiority Complex

THE CURIOUS THING about the genuine "inferiority complex" is that the victim may not either consciously feel or act as if he were inferior. Indeed, his friends may think that, if anything, he suffers from a "superiority complex."

I once knew a woman of this sort. In the Women's Society of which she was a member she would have been permanent President if she could have had her way. When she was not President she had to manage the organization, including the President, anyway. In the choir of which she was a member she had to sing the solos, direct the processional, and select the music. In the anthems she was always half a beat ahead of the choir. She bustled and pushed around, always keeping herself in the foreground. In her home she managed everything, including her meek little husband, who finally resented the situation so much that he walked out. But all of this behavior was merely compensation for deep but buried feelings of inferiority. I happened to know something about her childhood, and the conditions in her home which placed her in an inferior status against which she bitterly rebelled. Her life was a constant struggle to prove to others, and even more to herself, that she was not inferior. The sense of inferiority, which had become a repressed unconscious complex, dominated her behavior, and expressed itself in extreme sensitiveness and exaggerated self-assertion. But her behavior antagonized others and failed to bring her sufficient self-approval. She was a fundamentally unhappy woman.

"Complexes" are defined by Professor J. A. Hadfield as "psychological constellations . . . , which, owing to their painful or repugnant character, are *unacceptable* to the self." [1] They therefore tend to be forgotten, unconsciously repressed. But they go on working dynamically in the psyche nevertheless. Thus the sense of inferiority, so repugnant to the individual that it is repressed and lives only in the unconscious part of the mind, functions nevertheless, producing a variety of unpleasant consequences, only one of which is this compensatory aggressiveness which has been described.

There is much loose talk about the "inferiority complex" and it is important that we should understand better what it is. It is not just the ordinary "feeling of inferiority" which at times plagues all of us. It is much more deeply rooted, it is always disguised, and it is much more difficult to cure. The fact that it is buried in the unconscious makes it hard to get at and to treat intelligently.

What most of us have to struggle with at some time in our lives, and some of us most of the time, is a sense of

[1] From *Psychology and Morals,* by J. A. Hadfield. By permission of the publishers, Robert M. McBride & Company.

inadequacy, unworthiness, inferiority. Perhaps it would not be too much to say that everybody has had to struggle to overcome some feelings of inferiority, and it is a very painful experience indeed. We compare ourselves with others and woefully feel how far we come short; we criticize and are dissatisfied with our achievements; we feel that we lack ability or mental facility; we do not possess the social poise and graces of others; we doubt our competency to carry through some project or enterprise which our ambition stirs us to undertake. Consequently we are embarrassed, we feel that our behavior is mistaken or blundering, we get fits of despondency and depression, and we are altogether miserable. There are people that we admire immensely, and we want to be like them and to accomplish great things as they do. But we haven't got what it takes, and in the presence of these great ones we stand tongue-tied. Perhaps these great ones once felt the same way; and there may even be times now when they do. For the *feeling of inferiority* is not necessarily related at all to *actual inferiority*.

Indeed, this is true of both the genuine inferiority complex and of inferiority feelings—they do not necessarily indicate real inferiority at all. Feelings of inferiority, even those that get so deeply buried as to result in inferiority complexes, arise from quite other causes. It would be quite simple if the inferior person felt inferior and the superior person felt superior, but it doesn't work that way at all. The superior and inferior persons may, indeed, be aware of their superior or inferior qualities; but, on the other hand, the superior person may feel inferior and the inferior person superior.

Shakespeare showed profound psychological insight when he put into the mouth of Cassius the words:

> "The fault, dear Brutus, is not in our stars,
> But in ourselves, that we are underlings."

It is not the external accident of fate, nor the lack of personal attributes, that makes one feel inferior—an underling—but conditioning circumstances and the individual's reaction to them.

What, then, are the causes of inferiority feelings—these feelings of inadequacy and disadvantage that so distress and debilitate us?

First, there are the experiences of childhood which we have all passed through. The little child is born into an adult-dominated world. He cannot avoid comparing himself with the grown-ups. He is little; they are big. He wants his way; they have theirs. The grown-ups determine when and what he shall eat, what he shall wear, where he shall go. His inferiorities are concrete and tangible; they have to do with size and power. Not what he wants, but what the omnipotent parents decide, "goes" in his little world. When any contest of will arises and the child suffers almost inevitable defeat, the painful sense of inferiority is deepened.

These are, of course, only a few of the more obvious and tangible ways in which feelings of inferiority are developed; there are thousands of more subtle processes. In most cases, especially where parents are wise and educational methods are good, these influences do not have permanently crippling effects. But in some cases the foundation for a real neurosis is laid in the family, and all of us require time and experience to achieve complete emancipation and self-confidence. Alfred Adler bases his entire psychological theory upon this struggle against inferiority, most of it, but not all, rooting back in childhood experiences.

A second root cause of inferiority feeling is found in some sort of organ deficiency. In our civilization, by and large, woman occupies an inferior status; therefore Alfred Adler refers to the struggle against inferiority as "the masculine protest." But people crippled, lame, chronically ill, possessed of speech or sight defects, suffer manifest inferiorities as compared with normal people, and these inferiorities have their necessary psychological implications. The handicapped individual may give up in helplessness, use his inadequacy to gain pity and so be cared for by others. Or he may become bitter and resentful and develop into a most unhappy and perhaps even dangerous person. We all have seen many examples of both these reactions. Or he may face his handicap as a challenge and achieve his greatest success at the point of his greatest deficiency. Many of the greatest artists have had defective vision; many musicians, like Beethoven, have been deaf; many athletes have had to overcome physical handicaps—a friend of mine who became all-round track champion of Canada went into athletics in the first place because, as a boy, he was threatened with tuberculosis: many great orators, like Demosthenes, who practiced speaking with pebbles in his mouth, have suffered speech defects. One of the greatest orators I have ever known, the late Dr. J. A. McDonald, editor of the *Toronto Globe,* was a terrible stutterer. He never completely overcame it. I heard him once, addressing an audience of 6,000 men in Massey Hall, almost completely break down, but he went on to complete a powerful speech. While he was in high school and college his friends did everything in their power to dissuade him from his efforts to become a public speaker, but, instead, he seized every opportunity to make a speech. And he became one of the most able orators of his day on the American continent. The point is that when all the powers of one's personality are marshalled to fight at the point where one suffers real inferiority it may be at that very point that the greatest distinction is achieved.

A third cause of inferiority feelings may be poor health. Anaemia, glandular dysfunction, endocrine imbalance, liver disorder, or other illnesses may have such a depressing effect that the individual loses heart and feels inferior. He is unable to look out upon life with courage and resolution. He is disheartened and inadequate. The remedy, of course, is proper medical attention.

One effect of inferiority feelings, or of an inferiority complex, as has already been pointed out, is compensatory behavior in the form of excessive self-assertion, aggressiveness, domineering attitudes. The function of such attitudes is to demonstrate to others and to convince oneself that one is not inferior. But the reaction to inferiority feelings may be, and probably much more often is, precisely the opposite. One acknowledges inferiority, even when he is not actually inferior. He doesn't trust himself. He feels despondent, depressed, apathetic. He will not venture upon tasks for which he is fully competent. He is fearful of failure, which would be intolerable. He compares himself with other men, usually overestimating them and underestimating himself, and feels miserable and beaten. When he does make an effort it is with scant self-assurance. Consequently, on account of this sense of inferiority, not because of any real inferiority, he muffs the ball and watches someone else run off with it. Thus many a man makes a dismal failure of his life because of a quite unwarranted lack of self-confidence. He fails, even when he might succeed brilliantly, solely because he lacks trust in himself. His trouble is that, despite the good qualities he possesses, he is in his own estimation an "underling."

What is the cure for this unhappy condition? Is there any way out of it? What insights will psychology give us? What does religion have to say that may be of help? In his book *Psychology and Morals*, Dr. J. A. Hadfield says: "There are three principles of psychological and moral health: Know thyself; accept thyself; be thyself." [2] Here, perhaps, we shall find the way to the cure of these distressing feelings of inferiority and to the achievement of such self-respect that we may live comfortably with ourselves and usefully with our fellow-men.

"Know thyself" was the wise dictum of the ancient Greek philosophers. But, as the psychoanalysts have shown, it is

[2] P. 78.

not easy to know oneself. It requires both careful heart-searching and objective appraisal. And we are so prejudiced with regard to ourselves that we are reluctant to examine our deeper motivations, and it is, moreover, very difficult to stand outside ourselves, free of personal bias, and take an honest look. Furthermore, we have been so psychologically conditioned by our experiences in childhood and in society that the picture we have of ourselves is distorted and inaccurate. It is not our imagined selves, nor the selves that we think others believe us to be, nor the selves that we should like to be, but our real selves that we need to know. And, while thorough self-examination may show us to be worse in some respects than we like to think, it may also show us to possess many more assets than we have believed, particularly if, as a result of some unfortunate experiences, we have been conditioned to feelings of inferiority and inadequacy.

One can well believe the story of the salesman who, having failed miserably in an attempt to make a sale to a great industrialist, partly because of his tongue-tiedness and timidity in the presence of this giant of industry, caught sight of himself in a mirror as he washed his hands and saw quite a different person from the one he had imagined himself to be. "What's the matter with me?" he asked. "I've got two eyes, two ears, a nose, a mouth, reasonably broad shoulders. I have a better than average education. I know my product, and it's a good product. Besides, it's needed. This man who just turned me down needed it. I'm through being scared, and I'm going in to sell!" And, going on to his next prospective customer, he did sell him, and soon became one of the best salesmen on the staff of his firm.

Many people might well overcome their damaging self-depreciation if they would thus look at themselves. If we would "know ourselves" we need to recognize our assets as well as our liabilities. We should not let ourselves be hampered by feelings of inadequacy which have no basis in real fact.

Of course, as the Apostle says, a man should "not think more highly of himself than he ought to think," but neither should he indulge in unjust self-depreciation. Anything that limits his helpfulness and usefulness, not to say his happiness and health, is to be deplored; and severe inferiority feelings can have such deleterious effects. A man is not a worthless worm; he is a child of God—a creature of inestimable worth. "Are not two sparrows sold for a farthing?" Jesus asked, "and one of them shall not fall to the ground without your Father. . . . Fear ye not, therefore, you are of more value than many sparrows." "We are the children of God!" says the Apostle. How may one know himself to be a child of God? "As many as are led by the Spirit of God, they are the sons of God." In a general sense, all men are children of God the Father and Creator, but in a very special sense those are His children who are led of His Spirit. Any man, then, no matter how great or small his endowments and attainments, if he yields himself to the leading of God's Spirit, may know himself to be a beloved son of God. How can such a man think himself to be inferior or unworthy? "Know thyself?" Yes, know thyself a child of the living God, precious in His sight, not inferior, but of superlative value. How many men might gain confidence and power for daily living with such a vision of themselves.

Not only know thyself, but *accept* thyself. Accept ourselves with our present limitations, but also with our present powers and our vast potentialities. Humility is a proper attitude in view of the distance between our achievements and our possibilities. "God resisteth the proud, and giveth grace to the humble." But humility is not a sense of inferiority and pride is not a just estimate of oneself; indeed, it is precisely the sense of inferiority that prevents men from becoming what, by the grace of God, they might become, while pride brings self-satisfaction with present achievement and inhibits all effort to rise to the greater heights of unrealized potentialities. To accept *ourselves* will put an end to that competitiveness, that comparison of ourselves with others, out of which the sense of inferiority arises. Bill Smith is asked to know, accept, and seek to realize the potentialities of Bill Smith; he is not responsible for fulfilling the possibilities resident in the personality of John Jones. If a man accepts *himself* he need not worry about excelling others, or being excelled by others. The responsibility of the man in the parable who was given one talent, was not to accomplish the results that might be achieved by the men with two or five talents, but rather to do his best with what he had. The cause of his failure was that, instead of accepting himself and doing his best, he compared himself with the others and felt so inferior that he buried his talent; and the penalty he suffered was the loss of even the one talent that he had. That is precisely what happens to the man who feels so inferior that he does not put his own powers to work.

And *be* yourself. But be your *best* self, and refuse to settle for anything less. "To thine own self be true." There is plenty of room here for high achievement within the plan and purpose of God. It was many years ago that William James said that most men realize probably less than ten per cent of the potentialities with which they are endowed. One need not be a Leonardo da Vinci, a Napoleon Bonaparte or an Albert Einstein, to be worthy of respect, or to hold his own self-respect; but it is easy to see how easily a man may lose his self-respect if he is satisfied to live at only ten per cent of his powers. To be yourself means to be your best self, not your lowest self; to realize yourself at the highest level of achievement within your capacities; to live as becometh a child of God.

We have all had our struggles with inferiority. This sense of inadequacy has often weakened us and rendered us unhappy and despondent. But no one need feel inferior. We have whatever talents God has seen fit to entrust us with, and we should use them fully, without complaining that others are more highly endowed than we. And, accepting and using the gifts we have, we shall grow. What the future possibilities of growing children of God may be we cannot tell. "Now are we the sons of God, but it doth not yet appear what we shall be." The way out of our inferiority is by being our best selves now, and by moving on to the realization of those unexplored and unimagined possibilities which are resident in the personality of every child of God.

CHAPTER 10

Love Against Hate

"YE HAVE HEARD that it hath been said, 'Thou shalt love thy neighbor and hate thine enemy.' But I say unto you, 'Love your enemies.'"

That is an extraordinary statement that Jesus made. He was not satisfied to say negatively, "You shall not hate your enemy." Plato has Socrates say, in the *Crito*: "We ought not to retaliate or render evil for evil to anyone, whatever evil we may have suffered from him." But Jesus said positively: "Love your enemies, bless them that curse you, do good to them that hate you, and pray for them which despitefully use you and persecute you." That's very hard to do. And why should a man love his enemy? For any good he may hope to get out of it? Well, Jesus doesn't say, except as it may be implied in the motivation He suggests for doing good to one's enemy: "That ye may be the children of your Father which is in heaven"—a Father who makes His sun to shine and His rain to fall on the good and the evil alike. It is a perfection like that of the Father in heaven that is demanded.

What is implied in the statement, of course, is that this attitude which is demanded of men—that is, of love toward all men, even one's enemies—is the attitude of God. It is a statement about the moral order of the universe. If that is your attitude, you are on God's side, and the ultimate victory is yours. If that is not your attitude, but if rather you persist in hate, your life faces ultimate defeat.

Here, in these two antithetical emotions, love and hate, you have what Dr. Karen Horney calls "the basic conflict" which, if unresolved, results in neurotic division of the personality. This she illustrates by reference to the story of Dr. Jekyll and Mr. Hyde. "We see him on the one hand delicate, sensitive, sympathetic, helpful, and on the other brutal, callous and egotistical." [1] This basic conflict is of course rarely dramatized in such extreme form, but in many lives it is there in lesser degree. The struggle between love and hate goes forward desperately in our own souls.

Hate, fundamentally, is any feeling that tends to pull us away from or incite us to take action against, another. It is divisive. It breaks up homes, it sunders communities, it rends the fabric of society. It is closely related to and often arises from fear—we hate that which we fear. It is usually accompanied by anger. It is utterly incompatible with joy and peace. As Dr. William S. Sadler has said, "There is simply no way to get comfort and delight out of hate—it is truly the arch-demon of all the little devils who are subversive of joy and destructive of happiness." [2]

[1] Reprinted from *Our Inner Conflicts* by Karen Horney. By permission of W. W. Norton & Company, Inc. Copyright 1945 by the publishers.

[2] *The Quest of Happiness*, p. 288, by W. S. and L. K. Sadler. By permission of the publishers, Funk & Wagnalls Co.

GREENLEAF 5-3716

THE NIELSEN'S, INC.
1920 HARRISON STREET
EVANSTON, ILLINOIS

DATE_____ 19____

M_____

_____

_____

Hate, then, is an emotion which, in the first place, cripples and distorts personality. Mental clinics are replete with examples of the crippling effects upon the evolution of a child's personality of intense feelings of fear and hate. The child who hates either withdraws within himself to avoid all personal entanglements with a hostile world, or else strikes out violently against it. In either case the integrity of his personality is endangered. Or he may be so torn between love and hate for the same person—for a strange ambivalence of this nature is quite common—that the inner conflict becomes intolerable.

I have in my files the case record of a young Jewish woman, reared in a home where the affectional ties of the family were strong, and who was, further, constantly reminded that it was her duty to marry and give her parents grandchildren. If she was to fulfil her role that was essential. But her father died when she was fourteen, and her mother became ill and demanded her constant attention. Indeed, there was no one else to look after the mother. An older sister was married and had her own family to care for. So the girl, over several years, had no time for any pleasures or for the attention of young men who might be attracted to her, and moreover was engaged in a task which had many distasteful and even disgusting features. She was bound to her mother by love, yet came to hate her for depriving her of a chance to fulfil her role as it had been inculcated in her, and for requiring an attention which involved loathsome tasks. At last she broke under it and, after an attempt at suicide, had to be committed to a mental hospital. To the doctor she moaned, "My poor, dear mother, I love her and she suffered so much. But she had no right to take my life, my beautiful life. I hate her for it." Hate is, indeed, an emotion that can destroy the integrity of personality.

But hate not only cripples and distorts personality, it is destructive of the fabric of society. Evil propagates itself. Selfishness in one person calls forth selfishness in another. Hate calls forth hate in return. And the destruction of the home, of the community, and even of the world, may follow from it.

That is one of the terrible things about war—it releases such a flood of hate and distrust that the world society becomes torn and fragmented, and to bind it together again becomes an almost insuperable task. We live in a world now torn by fear and distrust and hatred, and to build a world community—as we must, if we are to live in peace, or even to live at all—represents a gigantic challenge not only to the minds, but to the hearts of men.

Is there any place for hate in the world? Yes, there is. Like fear, hate is a biological necessity. An individual incapable of hatred would view the most cruel and detestable conduct without resentment and would make no effort to remedy the situation. But hatred must be directed against hateful ideas and actions, not persons. If hatred is directed against persons, or races, or nations (as was done too frequently, for example, during the last war, by contemptuous newspaper references to the Japanese as "yellow monkeymen"), attitudes are developed which both distort personality and carry immense menace to our hopes of building a decent world.

It is possible to hate that which the enemy represents—provided it is something really destructive of human good —without hating the enemy. And that is what Jesus said. He didn't say, "You shall love what your enemy does," but "You shall love your enemy." And you can do that even while you oppose his purpose. I recall that when our son returned from his service with the Royal Canadian Air Force, shortly after the United States entered the war, I overheard a conversation which he had with some of his Chicago friends. One of them said, "When you were fighting the Germans, Chuck, you must have hated them." But he replied, "Why, no, I didn't hate them and very few of our fellows did. They were just other boys doing their job as we were doing ours." But that did not prevent his opposing what they were trying to do. It seemed to me during the war that the intensity of hatred increased with the distance from the fighting front. I do not say that no soldier hated the enemy; of course many did, perhaps most of them. But I do say that it is possible to hate the hateful thing without hating the doer of it. Indeed, it is possible to love him, in the sense in which Jesus used that word. We may desire and work for his incorporation into the world community which it is still our task to build. We shall have a bit more to say about that later.

And what is love? Love, in its simplest definition, is any feeling that tends to draw us toward another person and to seek his good, just as hate drives us away from or moves us to injure another. When one defines love in such terms it becomes evident that one can even love one's enemy. For love is not sentimentality; it is a basic attitude that eventuates in action.

A friend of mine once said, "Love God with all your heart? Love your neighbor as yourself? Love your enemy? But how can one love on command? Love is something beyond rational control. You either love a person or you don't, and often you can't tell why. Love is like the wind that bloweth where it listeth and thou canst not tell whence it cometh or whither it goeth. So is everyone that is in love." But is that true? If one means by love that sentimental attraction which a young man feels for his sweetheart that probably is true. But if one means by love what Jesus manifestly meant, then the case is different. You may then love even people you don't like. For love means placing the other person on an equality with one's self, and seeking his good as one does one's own. And that is an attitude that can be brought under rational control. In this sense one may love one's enemy; one may seek the enemy's ultimate good, even while one fights that which the enemy seeks to accomplish.

In Santayana's *The Last Puritan*, the vicar says to Oliver Alden: "I suppose you have been taught—and it is our Lord's doctrine—that to serve our neighbor and to love him is to serve and to love God. But that is only when you love and foster in your neighbor his participation in divine life, his approach to some sort of perfection. If you love him for his weakness, because he succumbs to you, or serve him in his folly, you are devoting yourself to the service of his vices; you are his worst enemy, as well as God's: and you hate his soul and destroy it." [3] In the same way, if we oppose our enemy's intention, if we frustrate the hateful thing he attempts to do—the imposition of tyranny, the ruthless extermination of those who oppose his will, for example—and, on the other hand, do everything in our power to bring his conduct into harmony with the divine purpose, to "foster in him the divine life," then we love his soul. Such action, and such an attitude, which seeks his ultimate good, is a matter altogether apart from "liking." It is much more profound, it touches far greater depths. And it is such love that is redemptive both of the individual and of the life of society.

Love, then, in contrast with hate which is divisive, is unitive. It integrates the inner life of the individual and it unifies the life of society. It expresses itself in mutuality, coöperation, participation, sharing. The wider and more inclusive the love—from family, through neighbor, to enemy—the more extensive its redemptive and integrative work. It means literally an extension of the self, so that, by empathy, one enters into and shares the hopes and aspirations of others and feels their needs, and those hopes and needs become one's very own. Take that celebrated period of life when one falls in love. The fulfilment of the interests and wishes of the beloved becomes the dominant desire of the one who loves; those wishes are his wishes. No longer

[3] From *The Last Puritan*, by George Santayana. By permission of the publishers, Charles Scribner's Sons.

self-sufficient as he once was, the welfare of the beloved is now his chief concern. And so the process goes on. Through love one becomes identified with one's neighbor—whether the neighbor be the person who lives next door or, as in Jesus' parable of the Good Samaritan, the hated alien—or with the superstitious and fear-ridden native in the heart of Africa; or with the enemy in war-time, who is, after all, a brother, and a member of the same family of God.

Only this inclusiveness of love can heal the world's divisions. Martin Niemoeller who spent the war years in a German concentration camp because he would not go along with the Nazis, tells us that: "During these twelve years we have learned, we Christians in Germany—and with what gratitude—that we were borne up and sustained in our loneliness by the prayers and concern of our brothers all over the world, interceding on our behalf with God. I shall never forget my old father's words during his last visit to me in the Gestapo office at the Oranienburg concentration camp. As he left he said: 'My child, the Esquimaux in Canada and the Bataks in Sumatra send you their greetings and are praying for you.'" We are members one of another, and it is love that makes us aware of that relationship, and leads us to appropriate action. Do you recall John Donne's words, often quoted since they were used by Ernest Hemingway on the fly leaf of his *For Whom the Bell Tolls?* "No man is an *Iland*, entire of it self; every man is a piece of the *Continent*, a part of the *maine*; if a *Clod* be washed away by the *Sea, Europe* is the lesse, as well as if a *Promontorie* were, as well as if a *Mannor* of thy *friends* or of *thine own* were; any man's *death* diminishes *me*, because I am involved in *Mankinde*: And therefore never send to know for whom the bell *tolls*; It tolls for *thee*."

Only in such loving attitude and action can be found the means of overcoming the evils of the world, and uniting the sundered world society. Somewhere must be found, not only individuals, but a nation with sufficient insight and spiritual dynamic to break the chain of hate and distrust, producing hate and distrust in return. A Chinese sage in the sixth century before Christ saw this possibility when he said: "I meet good with good, that good may be maintained; I meet evil with good that good may be created." And it was Jesus who said: "Ye have heard that it hath been said, 'Thou shalt love thy neighbor and hate thine enemy.' But I say unto you, 'Love your enemies.'" Only thus can this hideous and menacing chain of hate that will destroy us be broken.

And the one who does indeed commit his life to the way of love works with God, who at last will triumph. That is, further, what Jesus says. Love, not because the object of love is worthy, but love, that you may be children of your Father in heaven, who loves men, and serves men, and gives Himself for them, however unworthy they may be. His heart of love embraces all His children, and He bears their burdens and sins through all the weary years. By sharing that love, and by letting that love work through us, we may be sharers with Him in the redemption of the world. That is a love that cannot fail, and that can know no ultimate defeat.

"O Love That Wilt Not Let Me Go," is perhaps the greatest of all the hymns of the blind Scotch preacher and poet George Matheson.

The story of his life is an inspiring one, the record of a courageous struggle against many handicaps. When, as a young man, he found himself going blind, he was engaged to be married to an attractive and gifted young woman with whom he was deeply in love. He felt, however, that in fairness he should offer to release her and, to his heart-breaking sorrow, she accepted that release. It was then that he wrote this moving hymn. There was still left a love that would not let him go, but which would flood his life and make it richer and fuller; a light which, though his present torch was fading, would grow brighter and fairer; a joy that would find him in his deepest pain; and a cross to share with Christ which would bring redemption and endless life.

> O Love that wilt not let me go,
> I rest my weary soul on Thee;
> I give thee back the life I owe,
> That in Thine ocean depths its flow
> May richer, fuller be.
>
> O Light that followest all my way,
> I yield my flickering torch to Thee;
> My heart restores its borrowed ray,
> That in Thy sunshine's blaze its day
> May brighter, fairer be.

O Joy that seekest me through pain,
I cannot close my heart to Thee;
I trace the rainbow thro' the rain,
And feel the promise is not vain
That morn shall tearless be.

O Cross that liftest up my head,
I dare not ask to fly from Thee;
I lay in dust life's glory dead,
And from the ground there blossoms red
Life that shall endless be.

The ultimate triumph, whatever the present nameless tragedy, is with life and love, if we will but let the life and love of God work through us.

CHAPTER II

Faith Versus Fear

IT IS NOT too much to say that a haunting fear pervades the life of man today to a greater degree than has been the case in many generations. There are personal fears that agitate and disturb us. We are uncertain about and fear for the future of our civilization. A young couple said to me not long ago, "We are very doubtful about the wisdom, or even the fairness, of bringing children into the kind of world this is becoming." There is a basic sense of insecurity. This fear disturbs the relations of social groups, races and nations.

In a recent article in the *New York Times Magazine*—certainly not a red sheet, or even a yellow one—Brooks Atkinson, writing under the title "Faith, Not Fear, Must Move Us," said, "A kind of vague fear permeates the country now. . . . It poisons our capacity to think clearly. We are afraid of Soviet Russia which, ironically enough, is afraid of us. . . . If the Thomas Committee wants to find a real adversary in its search for un-American activities it might investigate the growth of fear in this country. On the evidence of history fear is un-American. America was settled by foreigners who were not afraid of work or danger.

At crucial moments America has been inspired by men who were not afraid of freedom." [1]

I want to look at this matter of fear, to inquire what are its sources, what can be done about it, and particularly what resources there are in our Christian faith to help us face and master our fears.

Fear arises, I will venture to say, from three causes. First, there are the fears that arise out of what the psychiatrists call "the unconscious"—out of our repressed impulses, anxieties, hidden desires. Second, there are fears which arise from ignorance and distorted thinking. And third, there are fears that have adequate causes. For this is a world in which there is much to fear. Let us look at these three forms of fear.

First let us look at these abnormal fears that plague the lives of so many people. There is no point in saying that these fears are imaginary. They have real causes, although the causes are often deeply buried in the unconscious recesses of the mind. They have been driven to these hiding places because they are so unwelcome, so distasteful, so intolerable that they cannot be faced. But they must be faced and understood if they are to be rooted out.

In my book *Getting Down to Cases* [2] I have told the story of such an abnormal fear. It was the case of a young farmer, married and with a growing family, healthy and strong, who on the occasion of a thunder storm, or in a

---

[1] From article, "Faith, Not Fear, Must Move Us," by Brooks Atkinson, in the *New York Times Magazine*, November 23, 1947. By permission of author and publisher.

[2] The Macmillan Company, 1942.

muddy field, was likely to become so overwhelmed with fear that he would rush to his mother's home, bury his face in her lap, and shudder and cry like a terribly frightened child. He knew the fears were irrational, but he simply could not overcome them. What lay back of them? Well, it took a long time to find out, and it was discovered almost by accident. First, he was the victim of complete lack of sex education—indeed, when, as a little boy, he had asked his father something about "the facts of life," his father became angry, told him that he ought not to think about such things, and that if he ever caught him in any dirty practices he would "take the hide off him." This, of course, served only to clothe the whole subject with both fascination and horror. Then, when he was about eight years old, an episode occurred in which a little neighbor girl was involved but which was of no serious consequence whatever, merely the expression of unsatisfied curiosity. But it had been interrupted by a severe and sudden thunder storm. The boy was terrified. God was roaring at him, threatening him, going to punish him. He took the little girl's hand and ran toward the house. She stumbled and fell, and he left her crying and shrieking. Unreasoning terror gripped him and drove him on. Somehow he got to the house and ran to his mother for protection and comfort, throwing his arms about her, weeping and shaking with fear. But all of this, except the terror of the storm and the muddy field through which he ran, was forgotten. The whole event was so painful that he wanted to forget it, and he succeeded completely. But the event, although

forgotten by his conscious mind, went on working nevertheless in his unconscious mind, carrying a tremendous
emotional charge. The fear was "displaced" on the incidental occurrences of thunder, storm and muddy field,
while the true cause of fear, too horrible to be thought
about, was repressed. It was not until all this was un-
earthed, until, in Freud's words, "the unconscious was
made conscious," that the grown man was able to deal
intelligently with his problem and proceed to the necessary re-education of his emotions.

Now, there are multitudes of people suffering from fears
of that sort—fears associated with events repressed and forgotten. A minister friend of mine is afraid of contamination
by touching a door handle or anything else that he thinks
may not have been thoroughly cleaned. He lives in constant fear. We have talked together for hours, but never
have been able to get at the roots of it. And many other
instances might be cited. Of course, the case I have given
is extreme, but in greater or less degree such fears, with no
adequate observable cause, plague many people.

Now let us look at the fears which arise from ignorance
and distorted thinking. In a recent article in *The Christian
Century* (April 21, 1948) Madame Helene Schweitzer,
who in 1912 set out with her husband, the famed Albert
Schweitzer, to found a Medical Mission in the heart of
French equatorial Africa, tells something of the problems
they face. "Consider," she says, "the superstition which
dooms motherless infants to death. Natives ascribe the
death of a young mother to evil spirits and pretend that

any woman who might dare suckle the orphan child gives herself and her own baby into the power of the same evil spirits. More than once it has happened at our hospital that a woman who overcame her fears and out of sheer Christian love fed a motherless baby was ill-treated by her husband and compelled to leave. If her own child should sicken or die, such a woman would almost certainly be put to death. Here, too, it is not only the inbred fear of evil spirits that the convert must overcome; she must brave the wrath of her husband and family." [3]

Are such fears, arising from ignorance and superstition, to be found in civilized society? It is the considered opinion of psychiatrists who are dealing with the fear-ridden all the time that our society is shot through with and seriously disabled by such anxious fears, compulsive hatreds, and unreasoning terrors. We are unable to think clearly because of them. Dr. Brook Chisholm, executive of the World Health Organization, writing recently in the *Survey Graphic*, said, "The only real threat left to man in that part of the universe known to him . . . is man himself. . . . He cannot use his highly developed intellect effectively because of his neurotic fears, his prejudices and fanaticisms, his unreasoning hates and his equally unreasonable devotions; in fact, his failure to reach emotional maturity, or mental health." [4] Like the spies sent out by

[3] From *The Christian Century*, April 21, 1948. By permission of the publishers.

[4] By Dr. Brook Chisholm, in *The Survey Graphic*, October 1947. Used by permission.

the Children of Israel wandering in the wilderness, to report conditions in the Promised Land, we see enemies stronger and more numerous than ourselves, enemy strongholds and forts built to the sky, and giants walking in the land, even though they are not there. We are all liable to be stricken with unreasoning fears.

But, as I have said, there are plenty of real causes for fear. And the capacity for fear in the presence of a real cause is a biological necessity. We could not survive without it. Recently there came a story from Akron, Ohio, of a year-old baby girl taken into a hospital for observation because, as the doctors said, "it had never felt pain and is not likely to." She cries when she is hungry or angry but never when she is hurt. The mother first noticed the baby's peculiarity when, at six months of age, she bumped her head badly on the floor and didn't seem to mind at all. Later she laid her hand on the hot stove and just laughed. Of course, anyone will see at once the danger in which that child stands. Not feeling pain, and consequently lacking fear, she will live constantly in imminent peril of her life.

There are real perils confronting mankind—perils from disease, from carelessness, from social unrest, from nationalistic pride and ambition, from Communism, from war, and multitudes of other causes. And if we do not fear these perils and meet them intelligently and deal with them purposively, we face disaster. But this sort of fear we can handle. It is the causeless fears, the neurotic fears, the fears that arise from ignorance and distorted thinking, that carry the greatest threats to man's happiness, and, indeed, to his very existence.

The question that is naturally asked is: How, then, shall I deal with my fears? What can I do about them? Certainly no one wants to go about weakened and incapacitated by fear if it can be avoided. "Fear is torment," as the Scriptures say, and such torment is, if at all possible, to be avoided.

First, then, with regard to fears arising out of experiences, wishes, impulses which have been repressed and buried in the unconscious. The answer is that, if possible, competent help should be secured. It is no more disgrace to see a psychiatrist than it is to see a surgeon. The trouble is that such help is not easily obtainable. Dr. William Menninger who, as Brigadier General, was in charge of the army's psychiatric services during the war, is authority for the statement that only about ten per cent of the needed trained psychiatric personnel is actually available.

Still, something can be done. Talking the matter through with an understanding friend may help one achieve insight. The case to which reference has been made was handled by a minister. And, even though one may never penetrate to the heart of his trouble, one may achieve a faith which will free him from the paralysis of fear. According to Dr. J. A. Hadfield, one of the greatest living psychotherapists, there are two ways in which these buried fear-complexes may be resolved. One is by psychological analysis. The other is by religious faith. There may take place "such a revolution of soul that . . . those emotions which we attached to morbid things are aroused to attach themselves to the new idea."⁵ This, of course, is what occurs when a man is enabled to say, "I will trust in the Lord and not be afraid." "The Lord is my light and my salvation; whom shall I fear? The Lord is the strength of my life, of whom shall I be afraid?"

With regard to the second kind of fear of which we spoke—fear arising from ignorance and distorted thinking—the answer to the question as to how one may rid himself of it is: by more careful, thorough, objective thinking; by taking into account all the facts, and by thinking with one's mind rather than with one's emotions, prejudices and superstitions.

I referred a little while ago to Madame Schweitzer's article dealing with the fears of the African natives. Dr. Schweitzer himself was considered by the Missionary Society which supported his work to be too unorthodox to be permitted to preach, and was limited to his medical work. But later he was allowed to preach. When asked once what, with his critical outlook on theology, he found himself able to preach to these simple folks, he replied, "Oh, these people are born scared, live scared, and die scared of evil spirits. I limit myself to preaching to them that in spite of all appearances to the contrary, behind all the seeming mystery and cruelty of life, there is not terror but love, the Father of Jesus Christ."

What we need, then, in order to deal with this problem, is to rid ourselves of our prejudices, superstitions and igno-

⁵ From *Psychology and Morals*, p. 82.

rance by thorough, rigorous, objective thinking. We are to love and worship God with our minds as well as with our hearts. And we must cultivate a robust faith in the ultimate goodness of God.

And, with regard to the fears that have real causes, well, we can handle them. If we face them, recognize them for what they are, and deal with them intelligently, they will not overwhelm us.

A study was made of the widespread panic that accompanied Orson Welles' broadcast of his adaptation of H. G. Wells' story of the invasion from Mars. He told the story as if it were a newscast and as occurring as he related it, and he located it in New England. As he told this story of these monsters wading rivers, kicking over houses, crushing all resistance, utterly impervious to all attempts to hinder their progress, great numbers of people were terrified. Automobile drivers ran their cars into ditches, men seized rifles and ran out to meet the invaders, people actually died of heart attacks. And all this fear and panic arose from an imaginary source which men felt themselves unable to cope with. But when the broadcast came of the attack on Pearl Harbor there was no such panic. Certainly there was fear and alarm. But this was something they could understand and handle. It came within the compass of their experience, and they knew what to do about it.

My friend Ted Hume, son of a famous missionary doctor and himself a Congregational minister, who was killed while flying on a mission of mercy in the early years of the war, wrote a little prayer in 1941. It ran:

> Grant us courage to change what can be changed for Thy
> purposes;
> Grant us patience to endure what cannot be changed;
> And grant us grace to know the one from the other. AMEN.

Well, God does give us courage and patience to endure
what cannot be changed.

Certainly we should do what we can to rid the world
of those real causes of fear that surround our lives—fear of
famine and pestilence, fear of social unrest and war. Now
that we know, for example, as one eminent scientist has
phrased it, that "the universe is inflammable" we can take
steps to prevent the conflagration—provided our neurotic
fears do not hinder us. As this same scientist said, we must
not let some fool set a match to this inflammable material.
Indeed, we must find ways to use the heat of that inflammable material to warm the hearts of men; we must use this
heat to generate the steam that will drive machinery to lift
burdens from the backs of men; we must harness this
energy to meet fully, as it can, the economic needs of men
the world around, and thus eliminate one of the basic
causes of war. As Dr. Hadfield, to whom I referred before,
says, "There are two kinds of fear . . . the fear that paralyses and the fear that inspires. . . . Fear paralyses when
it offers no way of escape; it inspires when it is associated
with hope. A hare, suddenly surprised, is either temporarily
paralysed by fear, or stimulated to its topmost speed." We
need, desperately, in these days, that fear which will stimu-
late us to our topmost speed.

What I have tried to say with regard to all these forms

of fear is simply this: We need to rid our minds of our neurotic and ignorant fears; we need to face intelligently and courageously the real causes of fear; and we need to cultivate a robust faith in the ultimate goodness of God in whose hands our life rests—"God in whom we live and move and have our being." Faith is the antidote for fear.

First, we need to supplant fear with faith in our own hearts. In her poem "Conversation at Midnight," Edna St. Vincent Millay has the priest say:

"There is no peace on earth today save peace in the heart
At home with God. From that sure habitation
The heart looks forth upon the sorrows of the savage world
And pities them, and ministers to them; but is not implicated.
All else has failed, as it must always fail.
No man can be at peace with his neighbor who is not at peace
With himself; the troubled mind is a trouble maker." [6]

The one who has achieved that peace of heart which rests on faith in God is freed from fear. He can face any disaster, even the final one of death. He will say with the Psalmist, "Yea, though I walk through the valley of the shadow of death, I will fear no evil, for Thou art with me."

And, second, thus freed from fear in our own hearts, we shall be enabled to work with God for the elimination, so far as it can be accomplished, of all the removable causes of fear, assured that His purposes for human life are good. We may "rest in the Lord, and wait patiently for Him," knowing that "He will give us our heart's desire," provided only that our desires are good.

[6] From *Conversation at Midnight,* published by Harper & Brothers. Copyright, 1937, by Edna St. Vincent Millay.

CHAPTER 12

"The Voice of the Suppressed Good"

In his important book, *Psychology and Morals*, Dr. J. Arthur Hadfield says:

"So far as their purely psychological mechanisms are concerned, temptation and conscience are identical, for both are the voice of suppressed desires. Temptations are the voice of the suppressed evil; conscience is the voice of the suppressed good. When our impulses are aroused by the delights of evil, we are said to be tempted; when we awaken to the loveliness of the good, our conscience is aroused. . . . The man who is perfectly bad could not be tempted, nor the man completely good be conscience-stricken."[1]

The voice of conscience, then, is none other than the voice of the suppressed good which we have been reluctant to perform; the voice of duty which we have failed to heed. Perhaps the trouble has been, in part, in our uncertainty as to what was good, or in the utter transformation of our way of life which complete commitment to the good would require of us. But the voice of conscience keeps troubling us. We may try to ignore it; we may try to drown it; but if

[1] Pp. 37–38.

there is anything of good in us, it will continue to assert itself. The imperious sense of "oughtness" is part of our nature and will not be quieted or ignored.

This is well illustrated in the dramatic story of Paul's conversion. It is the record of a terrific inner conflict of conscience. The Apostle Paul had been reared strictly as a Pharisee. His early conscience required of him meticulous performance of the whole Jewish law. Anything that threatened that way of life was wicked and dangerous; it must be resisted. Consequently, when the Christians began their preaching, proclaiming that not obedience to that law but faith in Christ was the way of salvation, he bent his energies to defeat them. He hounded and persecuted them, seeking to bring them to trial. All of that he did in good conscience; such behavior, for him, was good.

It was at his feet that those who stoned to death the martyr Stephen laid their garments while doing their bloody work. It has been surmised that it was on that occasion, when Saul (for that was the name he bore then) saw the manner in which Stephen endured that shame and suffering that he began to doubt the rightness of his course. For Stephen, dying, cried, "Lord, lay not this sin to their charge!" It must surely have been in an attempt to drown the voice of a troubled conscience that Saul, in a frenzy of effort, "made havoc of the church, entering into every house, and haling men and women committed them to prison."

It was this stifled conscience which at last asserted itself, when, on his way to Damascus with authority and commission from the chief priests against the Christians, he was stopped on the road by a blinding vision which threw him to the earth, and he heard a voice speaking to him and saying, "Saul, Saul, why persecutest thou me? It is hard for thee to kick against the pricks." In this startling fashion the voice of the good, which he had been suppressing, arrested him, and this time he "was not disobedient to the heavenly vision." It was the turning point in his career. He ceased to kick against the pricks of the goad of conscience, but rather to follow its guidance.

I have listened to a good many psychiatric diatribes against ministers and religion on account of the guilt-inducing techniques which they are alleged to use in order to gain improvement of conduct. The sense of guilt thus induced, I have heard some of my psychiatrist friends assert many times, is a major cause of mental disturbance, ranging all the way from anxiety states to severe psychoses. And anyone who knows the facts is aware that the sense of guilt is, indeed, to be listed as perhaps the chief cause of functional mental disorder.

Well, what is the minister or the religious guide to do about this? Is he to tell people that things are all right when they are not right? To say "Peace! Peace!" when there is no peace? This whole matter is of such vast importance, and the issues at stake are so great, as to require careful and balanced consideration.

First, I would say that there are multitudes of people living on low ethical levels whose consciences must be aroused if they are ever to realize the potentialities with which they are endowed. It may be "hard for them to kick against the pricks," but, unless conscience does prick them, and they perhaps suffer severe emotional disturbance in the process, they will remain mediocre or positively bad when they might be serving man and God through high and worthy achievement.

Anton T. Boisen, speaking out of his experience as a chaplain in a mental hospital, has said:

"The more I see of the experiences through which our patients are passing, the more I am convinced that conflicts and disturbances are not necessarily evils, but merely incidental to a needed reorganization of personality. . . . Most men, even those who have had every advantage, go through life absorbed in the petty and trivial and the selfish and even in that which makes them loathsome in their own eyes, and forgetful of the great issues which are of enduring importance to themselves and to the race. It is the church's business to *save* such men, and that means to disturb their consciences with regard to the quality of the life they are living in order that they may turn and be made whole, and to do so before they perhaps develop symptoms which bring them to some such institution as ours." [2]

An untroubled conscience is a wonderful thing to possess, if it is justified. But a conscience that is untroubled when it ought to be troubled—when one's life is unworthy, when there are wrongs to be righted which we neglect, when evil is done and we stand by callous and uncaring—

[2] *The Journal of Religion*, January, 1927, pp. 76 ff. Used by permission.

then such an untroubled conscience represents moral blindness and a hardening of the heart which sets one on the road to hell.

The simple and inescapable fact is that, without a troubling of conscience and its consequent sense of guilt, there will be no improvement. If our souls are to be cured our consciences need to be disturbed about the inferior quality of our lives.

But the second thing to be said, and equally important, is that we must be sure that we are acting under the impulse of an enlightened conscience. We say, perhaps without sufficient thought, that a man ought to obey his conscience. But we know that all too often people conscientiously advocate all sorts of fads and follies, sometimes with dire consequences. I presume that most of those men who conducted the so-called "Holy" Inquisition, with its horrible tortures and burnings at the stake, did so in good conscience. They were intent on saving the souls of men by bringing them to accept the authority and the theological formulations of the Church. It was no pleasant task for Frenchmen to burn Joan of Arc, the savior of France, but she had been adjudged a heretic, dangerous to the Church and to the souls of men and, since she would not recant, she could not be permitted to live. And what about the Apostle Paul himself? In all good conscience, in those days before his conversion, he persecuted the Church. "I verily thought," said he at his trial before King Agrippa, "that I *ought* to do many things contrary to the name of Jesus of Nazareth. Which things I also did in Jerusalem: and many of the saints did I shut up in prison . . . and when they were put to death, I gave my voice against them."

One wonders, sometimes, if more harm has not been done through ignorance than through real intent of evil. The sense of "oughtness," the prodding of conscience, is terribly important. But too often the content of that which we feel we ought to do is determined by the social "mores," the uncriticized folk-ways, the prejudices and biases of our groups. Conscience, unfortunately, does not give intuitive insight into right and wrong. The determination of the better or the worse requires high intelligence and calls for critical evaluation of conduct in terms of probable social consequences. Certainly, a man ought to do what conscience directs him to do, but it should be an intelligently informed conscience, a conscience which is based upon critical examination of the issues, and which has sought the truth humbly and reverently in the presence of God. A man has not done his full duty when he has done what he feels that conscience directs, unless he has done everything in his power, through careful thought and prayer, to assure himself that what conscience directs is right and good.

Don't be afraid to trust your own mind in determining these issues. That is what God gave it to you for. You will recall the rhyme, said to have been written by a Harvard faculty member:

> Here's to the city of Boston,
> The home of the bean and the cod;
> Where the Lowells speak only to Cabots
> And the Cabots speak only to God.

Someone wrote it out and sent a copy to Dean Jones of Yale University who then penned another toast:

> Here's to the town of New Haven,
> The home of the truth and the light;
> Where God speaks to Jones in the very same tones
> He uses to Hadley and Dwight.

Well, that's a true insight. Certainly you will consider the opinion of others. But you do not have to depend on the dictum of pope or priest or professor. If you will use the mind that God gave you, and sensitively seek His leading, you may learn what is true and right.

And the third thing to say is that the following of an enlightened conscience—"a good conscience toward God"—is the way to happiness, usefulness and mental health.

At a psychiatric conference in Chicago a few months ago a psychiatrist had been expatiating on the manner in which the repression of organic impulses under the influence of a sense of guilt resulted in the formation of complexes and consequent mental illness. We are all familiar with that thesis. But one of the most eminent psychiatrists there, a man who had been working in the field for many years and was then teaching in the medical school of a leading American university, rose to say that the psychiatric profession had, in his judgment, been travelling on the wrong track for a long time. It is not the repression of impulse, he said, that causes the difficulty, but the attempted repression of conscience. It is conscience which differentiates man from the beast. It must be heeded if we are to have a decent human life. And it is the attempt to repress it in the interest of merely gratifying instinctual cravings that causes disintegrating inner conflict.

My own opinion is that this man was right. Moreover, I can quote Freud himself to support the view. "Civilization," he said, "was forged at the cost of instinct satisfaction." That is, instinct must be curbed, sublimated, redirected to ends socially higher, if we are to live as human beings, to say nothing about living as children of God. That means that conscience must not be repressed for it is, as Hadfield says, "the voice of the repressed good," and it will keep on speaking, troubling, disturbing us if we attempt to repress it, and sometimes with disastrous consequences.

I have seen many of the case records of a friend of mine who served for some time as psychological consultant in a gastro-intestinal clinic. One of these cases was that of a successful businessman who had been strictly reared as a Methodist, and who, although he now rarely attended church, had been unable to rid himself of his Methodist conscience. He was a widower who, because of the insistence of his demanding and possessive mother and his two spinster sisters that he make his home with them, did not re-marry. But he established a love nest, as much as a place of refuge from his mother as for any other reason. His Methodist conscience, however, would not allow him to rest content with this arrangement, and he was so terribly torn by inner conflict that he developed stomach ulcers, severe mucous colitis, and heart palpitations. He became a physical wreck. No medication could help him.

"The voice of the repressed good" had to be heeded. It was not until he cleaned up the whole mess of his inner life and organized his life in terms that conscience required, that he was restored to health.

"It is hard for thee to kick against the pricks," said Jesus in Paul's vision. The ox who kicks against the pricking of the goad only suffers in consequence. It is so with us when we kick against the pricking of the goad of conscience. A well-instructed conscience should be our guide, not our goad, and, when it is, it will lead us on to a happy and useful life. Henry Wright of Yale used to challenge students with a life decision card which, whatever our maturity, might well indicate the terms of a life commitment which will bring happiness and success:

"I will live my life for God, for others rather than for myself, for the advancement of the Kingdom of God rather than for my personal success. I will not drift into my life work, but I will do my utmost by prayer, investigation, meditation, and service to discover that form and place of life work in which I can become of the largest use to the Kingdom of God. As I find it I will follow it under the leadership of Jesus, wheresoever it takes me, cost what it may."

CHAPTER 13

Masks and Mirrors

WE ALL wear masks—masks intended to hide our loneliness, our fears and hopes and misgivings; sometimes masks intended to deceive others into thinking more highly of us than we deserve; and, quite often, masks by which we try to deceive even ourselves.

There is a dreadful story in the Old Testament about a seige of the city of Samaria by Ben-hadad, king of Syria. The city was reduced to such horrible straits of deprivation and starvation that, we are told, "an ass's head sold for four score pieces of silver, and the fourth part of a scab of doe's dung for five pieces of silver." The people were even reduced to cannibalism. One day, as the king of Israel passed by upon the top of the wide city wall, clad in his royal robes, a woman cried to him, "Help, my lord, O King!" The king asked what help he could give her, when the barn floor and the wine press were both empty. And the woman told her pitiful and horrible tale. Starved, she and another woman had agreed to kill and eat, first her son, and, later, the other woman's son. She had destroyed her son and they had devoured him, but now the other woman had hidden her son and would not surrender him. And when the king heard these words, we are told, he rent his royal garments, "and the people looked, and, behold, he had sackcloth within upon his flesh." There you have it: the outward show of royalty and pomp, within, and known only to himself and God, the tokens of shame, sorrow and humiliation.

This tendency not to reveal our true selves to others, or even acknowledge our true selves to ourselves, arises from the strange complex of elements that make us what we are. On the one hand, we are the inheritors from our animal ancestry of biological urges and organic hungers, capacities for lust, fear, rage and hate, which we often find it difficult to hold in check and of which we are sometimes ashamed. On the other hand, we are possessed of godlike powers—of hopes and dreams, aspirations after goodness and brotherliness and fellowship with God—which we find it hard to achieve. Yet, deeply, we want to be our best. We should like others to think the best of us. And we want to think well of ourselves. So, we tend to wear masks. But our destiny, we are sure, is something more than the wearing of a mask. It is the achievement of the divine potentialities that are ours as children of God.

In his important book, *The Human Mind*, Dr. Karl A. Menninger has pictured this struggle within the human personality under the figure of a play. The actors are the ideas and desires, while the stage manager is the "ego-idea"—the "censor," the psychoanalyst calls it—that aspect of the personality which approves or disapproves the ideas or desires which shall find overt expression. But all the actors want to act, and hang around the wings trying to get on the stage. The actors have to take their turns, and are permitted to appear when the time comes by the stage-manager, but most of them would like to "steal the show" and remain there all the time. Others of these ideas and desires are poor actors, unacceptable to the stage-manager, and are thrown out and never allowed to appear—they are "repressed," to use the psychologists' term. They are driven into the unconscious. But, to quote Menninger, these repressed actors "may trick the stage-manager by disguising themselves in various costumes and masquerading as proper actors of the show. They are never wholly proper, and the keen eye may detect their identity and trace their origin. But the average playgoer (the ordinary person) will think only that the play is here and there a bit shabby or clumsy or strange." [1] Psychoanalysis, Dr. Menninger points out, is concerned with a study of the various modifications and disguises which cloak the original intentions, cloaking them from the person himself even more successfully as a rule than from the outside world (pp. 269–70). The author then goes on in a long chapter to examine these disguises and masks which the human desires assume in order to get on the stage of overt expression.

Very often, as Dr. Menninger says, these disguises deceive the individual involved more than they do the onlooker. In his book *The Madman: His Parables and Poems*, Kahlil Gibran tells a story of The Sleep Walkers:

[1] From *The Human Mind*, by Karl A. Menninger. By permission of the publishers, Alfred A. Knopf, Inc.

"In the town where I was born lived a woman and her daughter, who walked in their sleep. One night, while silence enfolded the world, the woman and her daughter, walking, yet asleep, met in the mist-veiled garden. And the mother spoke, and she said: 'At last, at last, my enemy! You by whom my youth was destroyed—who have built up your life upon the ruins of mine! Would I could kill you!' And the daughter spoke, and she said: 'O, hateful woman, selfish and old! Who stand between my freer self and me! Who would have my life an echo of your own faded life! Would you were dead!' At that moment a cock crew, and both women awoke. The mother said gently, 'Is that you, darling?' And the daughter answered gently, 'Yes, dear!'" [2]

Most of our masks, of course, do not disguise as unpleasant realities as are indicated in this parable. But the parable does suggest the subtlety with which the human mind works in repressing those impulses and desires which are unacceptable, and yet the manner in which they will find expression when the stage-manager—the censor, or the ego-ideal—is not on the job.

It is important that we should know our real selves—really and honestly understand ourselves with masks removed. We need to know, and understand, and accept, not the mere surface phenomena of our lives, but the deep-lying motivations and desires. Then we shall be able to manage our lives better. A minister friend of mine who

[2] From *The Madman: His Parables and Poems* by Kahlil Gibran. (Quoted by Karl A. Menninger in *The Human Mind*). By permission of the publishers, Alfred A. Knopf, Inc.

underwent psychoanalysis said afterward to his analyst, "Now that I've had an honest look at many of my real motivations, I am a bit shocked. I don't know how I shall ever respect myself again!" But his analyst said, "When you think it over, you'll not respect yourself less because you know yourself better. You will see what aspect of your personality has won out after all. And you will have a great deal more understanding and sympathy for other people who fail. You will be a better man."

It was with the deep-lying motivations of men, rather than with their overt behavior, that Jesus was concerned. The Pharisees He called "whited sepulchres"—sepulchres are a sort of mask—which appear to men to be beautiful outwardly, but within are full of corruption and dead men's bones. "Out of the heart of men," He said, "evil thoughts proceed." Condemnation in the sight of God does not wait upon the actual yielding to lust. "He that looketh upon a woman to lust after her hath already committed adultery in his heart."

The story is told that when the moving pictures were first shown in the American West, the cowboys shot the screen full of holes when the villain started to drag off the heroine. If the cowboys were to stop the villain, however, they should have turned their bullets on the projection room, the source from which the picture was thrown on the screen. So it is with our human behavior, the source is in the heart of man, and it is this source of motivation that God considers. "Man," said Jesus, "looketh upon the outward appearance, but God looketh upon the heart." That is, God is not concerned merely with the outward correctness of a man's life, the extent to which his behavior conforms with the requirements of law. He is concerned about whether good or evil, love or hate, purity or lasciviousness, reign in the inner recesses of the mind and heart. Before God we are what we are. We stand unmasked. And we need His help if we would really know ourselves.

There is an interesting statement in James' Epistle. The man who is a hearer but not a doer of the Word, the Apostle James says, "is like a man who looks in a mirror at the face that nature gives him, and then goes off and immediately forgets what he looked like." That is like so many men. They get some sort of hasty look at themselves in some mirror—in a bit of psychological exploration, or in the Bible, or through the comment of a friend—but, not being committed to a search for the truth and an irrevocable following of it, they go away and think of themselves in terms of the mask which they consistently wear. But, the Apostle goes on to say, he that is a doer and not a mere hearer of the Word looks in the mirror and finds it a "perfect law of liberty." He is blessed in his work.

We need to get a good look at ourselves, and then not forget what we look like. A young clergyman observed that every day a prominent surgeon, chief of staff in a great city hospital, stopped in his church on his way home from his duties for a few minutes of prayer and meditation. One day the clergyman ventured to approach the surgeon and said,

"I suppose you come to pray for your patients." "Yes, somewhat," the surgeon replied gruffly, "but not mainly; I come to have a good look at myself." We all need to do that, to search our own hearts in the presence of Him who "sets our secret sins in the light of His countenance."

"O, wad some Power the giftie gi'e us to see oursel's as ithers see us," sang Robert Burns, the Scotch poet. Dr. Lieper tells us that an American gentleman who was taking the channel steamer from Fusan in Korea to Nagasaki, some time before the war, found himself sharing a stateroom with an Oriental gentleman. After the steamer had left port the American went to the purser, and said, "I don't like the looks of that Jap in my stateroom. I want you to put my valuables in your safe." "All right, sir," said the purser, "he brought his down about half an hour ago!" Perhaps both were wrong in their misgivings, but, if they both learned what had gone on, each would know how he appeared in the other's eyes.

But it is more important that we should see ourselves as God sees us. As Dr. Albert C. Outler says, "To know what we really are is the first step toward becoming what we ought to be. It was when the prodigal son came to *himself* that he made the decison that put him on the road back to his father's house." J. S. Hoyland has written this little prayer:

O Thou who dost deliver us from ourselves,
Purge us today from all that is of the beast within us,
Drive from us all the leering and plausible devils of sin,

Those devils which have been born within us of the sore
    struggle upward of our race,
And which in the past, by our own grievous fault, we have
    pampered and encouraged.[3]

There is an important point in that prayer. We are not
responsible for the animal hungers and passions which we
have inherited. But we are responsible if we have pampered and encouraged them. That is our own grievous
fault. Certainly they are the essential driving forces of
human life; but they are to be made our servants, not our
masters. They are to be made the driving forces for the
achievement of those values and purposes which we should
cherish as children of God.

Where are we to find mirrors in which we may clearly
see ourselves? Well, that is one of the services which modern depth psychology has done for us. The psychoanalysts
have driven into the deep, dark, hidden and fiercely guarded
recesses of the unconscious mind, and dragged out the
motives that operate there. Freud suggests that most of
what we find there is slimy and unpleasant, but Jung finds
there also much that is good, that seeks high and noble
ends. At any rate, whatever is there, we need to know about
it, if we would truly know ourselves and manage our
lives well.

But the Bible long ago anticipated what depth psychology has revealed. "The heart is deceitful above all things,
and dreadfully wicked," said the prophet Jeremiah. And

[3] From *A Book of Prayers Written for Use in an Indian College*, by
J. S. Hoyland: The Society for Promoting Christian Knowledge.

Jesus, too, pictured the heart of man as the source from which come all manner of evil things—"murders, adultery, fornication." But love and goodness also are there, and "out of the good treasure of his heart" a man may "bring forth good things." It is the "pure in heart" who see God.

If we will but remove our masks and look in clear mirrors we shall be started on the way to becoming what we ought to be. We need to recognize the possibilities of evil within us, and, as the Book of Common Prayer says, "not cloak them." We should not pretend to be other than what we are. Perhaps some of us need to come to a genuine conviction of sin, which will be the first step toward our regeneration. But we need, also, to recognize within ourselves the possibilities of strength and the potentialities for good which are there, and to determine to live up to our full stature instead of being content with trivial things. Perhaps Jesus, looking upon one of us today, might see possibilities far beyond our present achievement. You remember his assessment of Simon—poor, uncertain, impulsive, sometimes terror-stricken, Simon—Simon scared near to death by a maid's taunt, "Thou art one of them!" replying with oaths, "I never knew Him!" It was this Simon to whom Jesus said: "Thou art Peter, a Rock! and upon this rock I will build my church." He saw the potentialities in an apparently weak and utterly unreliable man. And there may be like potentialities in us if we will but look, unmasked, in that mirror of God's truth, which shall be for us "the perfect law of liberty."

CHAPTER 14

Your Religion and Your Health

WHEN THE PSALMIST said: "Bless the Lord,
O my soul . . . who forgiveth all thy iniquities; who
healeth all thy diseases," he anticipated by many centuries
the findings of modern psychosomatic medicine. As shown
over and over again in cases cited by Dr. Flanders Dunbar,
perhaps America's leading authority in psychosomatic medicine, in her recent book *Mind and Body*,[1] feelings of guilt
cause such terrific inner tension and turmoil that bodily
functions are disturbed and frequently serious organic illness results. If illness of this sort is to be cured, the attack
must be made upon the emotions and the sense of guilt
removed. Thus, the assurance of the forgiveness of one's
iniquities may frequently have as its happy consequence
the healing of disease. Dr. Dunbar's own cases not only
indicate the causative factors in guilt feelings and disturbed
emotions, but also demonstrate the curative effects of relieved guilt-feelings, anxieties and fears.

In my own *Getting Down to Cases*[2] the stories of several people are told which illustrate the same point. There

[1] Published by Random House.
[2] Published by the Macmillan Company.

is a church deacon, widely respected and admired in both church and community, who fell ill with high blood pressure, colon infection, kidney disorders, and other complications. When his case did not respond to medical treatment the physician enlisted the aid of the deacon's pastor, and there the overplus, which the doctor suspected, was discovered. There had been some wild episodes in the deacon's young manhood, before his conversion, and now, one of the women with whom he had gone astray had returned to town and was trying to see him. There were other causes for anxiety. And now the deacon, fearful that the news would get out and run riot through the community, and deeply sensitive of the evil in his past life, was plunged into such fear, shame and remorse, that he felt himself threatened with the loss of the respect and affection of his friends and, what was worse, shut out from the presence of God. This was the situation that had to be dealt with before any improvement in health could be expected. Another case was that of a lovely and charming young woman who, although apparently happily married, neglected all the responsibilities of home-making and refused her husband children, until he, fed up, left her. Then, humiliated and really sick with heart and intestinal disorders, she took to her bed. It was not until, under skilful guidance, her repressed guilt-feelings were brought into into the open and honestly faced, with a resulting fundamental readjustment of her attitudes and behavior, that health was restored— and, happily also her husband recovered.

This does not mean—and Dr. Dunbar, to whom I have

referred, emphasizes this—that all diseases are caused by emotional disturbance. There are malarial infections, typhoid, amoebic dysentery, and all kinds of diseases that require quite orthodox medical treatment. You can't set a broken leg with psychological or spiritual treatment alone. But an astonishing number of illnesses with organic symptoms, and even organic derangement, have psychological causes. The late Dean Irving S. Cutter, of Northwestern University Medical School, was authority for the statement that probably considerably more than fifty per cent of the patients who visit physicians' offices have psycho-genic illnesses—that is, sicknesses that originate in disturbed mental and emotional states even though the symptoms are organic. Psychosomatic medicine (and "psychosomatic" is just a $64 word for "body-mind") recognizes that you cannot effectively treat a sick body (soma), when the sickness originates in the mind (psyche), unless you attack also the mental and emotional causes of the disorder. You must treat the whole person, not simply a liver, or a heart, or a colon.

And what is the nature of these disturbed emotional states? Just ordinary fears, worries, feelings of inadequacy, and above all guilt-feelings, especially when, because they militate against our self-respect, they are repressed. They may be driven from consciousness, or at least to its periphery, but they go on working dynamically in the individual's psyche nevertheless. As Helen Bassett, in her *Mental Health in the Community*, reminds us, there are few nervous conditions in which intense feelings of fear,

shame, guilt and remorse do not play a major creative
role.

This brings us to the question of mental health, since
mental ill health is seen as a major cause of bodily disorder.
It is with the mental health of the sufferer that the prac-
titioner of psychosomatic medicine is primarily concerned,
although, at the same time, he gives whatever ordinary
medical care the case may require. And how is mental
health to be described?

As mental health is now being conceived, it is not
thought of as merely the absence of distressing symptoms—
guilt, fear, remorse, etc.—in these unhappy symptoms. But
even that is a somewhat negative statement. The World
Health Organization has defined health in these terms:
"Health is a state of complete physical, mental, and social
well-being and not merely the absence of disease or in-
firmity." Mental health, then, will be a state of complete
mental well-being, and not merely the absence of mental
disorder. Such a condition of complete mental well-being
can be achieved only as one is correctly adjusted to the real
world—physical, mental, and spiritual—in which our human
lives are enacted; and such an adjustment requires as a
prerequisite an understanding and acceptance of that world.
Just as lack of understanding and adjustment, or any attempt at flight from this reality, results in disturbed emotional states, so a correct understanding and adjustment, a
fearless and intelligent facing of this reality, issues in
healthy emotional states—inner peace, happiness, confidence, and facility in moving toward adequate life goals.

Now, it seems to this writer that too much discussion of mental health, just as of physical health, has occupied itself with a discussion of symptoms rather than with causes. We have told people to get rid of their fears and guilt-complexes and to cultivate an attitude of hope and confidence, but have failed to raise the more fundamental question as to why people are obsessed with fear and guilt and are unable to face life with courage and good cheer. We have been applying superficial remedies to surface phenomena— like applying a salve to sores when we ought to have been seeking the deeper-lying disorder that causes the sores, and dealing with it. The sores will disappear when the disorder which causes them is cured. So it is with these unhappy emotional states. Why are men guilty and fearful? Why do they lack confidence? Of what basic maladjustments are these unhappy states the symptoms? These are the questions which we ought to ask. And, further, we should inquire what can be done to assist that fundamental readjustment to life and to the real world which must be achieved if men are to find fulfilment and happiness.

In this respect it seems that religion has been wiser than medicine. It is true that, by and large, religion has been short on diagnosis. It has labeled every inadequacy and failure as "sin" without too careful an examination of the nature and causes of these failures, with the result that too many "sinners" have felt that they have not been understood. On the other hand, medicine has concerned itself too much with symptoms and too often has tried to relieve the symptoms by such inadequate advice as that of lowering the conscience threshold—telling patients that their troubles are caused by hyper-conscientiousness, and that they must not expect too much of themselves. Religion, on the other hand, with all its inadequacies, is centrally concerned with that fundamental adjustment that it is necessary for men to achieve if they are to be made whole. They are told that they must come to terms with that ultimate Reality in which men live, and move, and have their being, and bring their thoughts and purposes into willing harmony with it if they are ever to find life's true fulfilment and, consequently, any lasting serenity and peace.

What I have to say is quite frankly based on the Christian view of life, and its source, meaning and destiny. If one takes a materialistic view of life it will be difficult indeed to find any meaning in it—life is a cosmic accident involving numberless frustrations which we endure as best we can until we meet ultimate defeat in death. If, on the other hand, the Christian view of life is true—that the source of our being is God, and that the true fulfilment of life is the discovery and doing of His will which is our good, then life takes on dignity, meaning and value. We can endure temporary frustrations, disappointments and defeats; we can learn through suffering; we can contribute to the discovery and more perfect doing of God's will; and we can live our lives in serenity and faith, believing that we move forward toward a goal which is at once man's highest good and the unshaken purpose of God.

This is not rank sentimentalism, as some would suggest. Indeed, if outcomes in terms of personality achievement and social progress are to be the criteria by which one judges the correctness or error of one's interpretation of the meaning of life, this is utter realism. When Arnold Toynbee, in his *Civilization on Trial*,[3] came to list the greatest benefactors of mankind, he did not list the world conquerors, much less the great skeptics, but the founders of the great religious faiths of mankind: "Confucius and Laotse; the Buddha; the Prophets of Israel and Judah; Zoroaster, Jesus, and Muhammed; and Socrates." It is the men of faith—faith in a good and wise God, whose will gave meaning and direction to life—who, in the long look of history, prove to be the benefactors of all men in all generations. The ethic associated with all these religions is very similar, and the interpretation of life as the fulfilment of the purpose of a good and loving God is closely parallel.

But Christianity, this writer is convinced, possesses unique insights of the greatest value. It maintains that the God of the Universe is the kind of God whose nature shines in the face of Jesus Christ—the Father of all mankind, an Eternal Justice tempered with Mercy, whose heart of love embraces all His children. Behind all the mystery and even the torment of this life, it maintains, a good Purpose prevails, a Will which has something in common with our human wills, which we may discover and do.

> Our wills are ours, we know not how;
> Our wills are ours to make them Thine.

[3] Published by the Oxford University Press.

This will is our good. To discover it is to discover the meaning of life. To do it is to find our true liberty. To become the instruments of this Eternal Purpose is to achieve dignity and worth. The person who has thus found life's meaning, value, proper direction and support lives serenely, not with a false serenity which comes from evading life's storms and problems, but with a true serenity which is able to live with and work through them. Faith, hope, love, become the dominant characteristics of such a life.

Now, these positive, constructive attitudes and emotions have immense value for health, just as the negative emotions of fear, anxiety and guilt have damaging effects. The latter are the emotions that control the sick mind; the former are the emotions of the healthy mind. And we humans are so put together that a healthy emotional life promotes the general health; while unwholesome emotions menace health. It is quite true that some forms of religion utilize overmuch the negative emotions in order to gain control of conduct; and, unquestionably, there is a place for fear and guilt in leading people to avoid or leave those forms of conduct which are unworthy and oppose the will of God. What Christianity insists upon is that this is a moral universe, based on the will of God, and that the fulfilment of that will is our good, while opposing it is our evil. Thus, the inner conflict which the sense of guilt brings may be a necessary phase in the process by which life is brought into proper adjustment with God's will. But the powerful, dominant emotions, the healthy attitudes, which characterize the Christian life, and which contribute to the complete health of the individual—spiritual as well as physical—are those of faith and hope, confidence and love. Moreover, the most admirable conduct is not that to which one is driven by fear, but that which is the normal expression of love.

When the Psalmist, in giving thanks to God, placed together the forgiveness of sins and the healing of disease, he expressed a sound psychological insight. The assurance of forgiveness is often a long step toward healing. But one needs to enter a caveat here. It is not that sickness is punishment for sin—that is a very ancient but false idea. Jesus' disciples asked their Master concerning a blind beggar by the wayside, "Master, who did sin, this man or his parents, that he was born blind?" And Jesus replied, "Neither did this man sin, nor his parents." Sickness is not punishment for sin. But there is a close relationship between sin and much sickness. The sense of guilt is one of the major forms of that emotional disturbance which upsets normal bodily functions, and so contributes directly to ill health.

What, then, shall we do about it? Some psychiatrists try to lessen the sense of guilt by telling their patients to forget about it, or by suggesting that they are victims of an oversensitive conscience and that they hold themselves to too high standards. Certainly ethical standards sometimes need revision—there are people, for example, who think all thoughts of sex are evil, as a consequence of rigid, puritanical and ignorant instruction when they were children, and who consequently are totally unfitted for marriage. The sinfulness of "concupiscence" has been much overemphasized. The text, "Behold I was shapen in iniquity and in sin did my mother conceive me," has been so misinterpreted as to cause unnecessary guilt-feelings. But, for the most part, the cure of the sense of guilt is not to be found in the lowering of standards. The instructed and sensitive conscience is the source of all moral advance. Yet we all sin, and we all, at times, feel guilty, and ought to feel guilty.

It is the Christian doctrine of the forgiveness of sins that holds the cure. "Bless the Lord, O my soul, who forgiveth all thy iniquities," said the Psalmist. Trust in a God who knows our frailties and remembers that we are dust: who freely and fully forgives on condition that we truly repent and turn from our iniquities; who endues us with the power of a new life when we look to Him for help—here is the remedy for the sense of guilt, far more potent than any effort to forget that which we never can forget, or to make ethical compromises which bring disaster to the individual and peril all moral advance.

There is a story in the New Testament that surely gives a true insight into the mind of God. A woman was brought before Jesus who had been taken in adultery, caught in the very act. The Pharisees, evidently, hoped to entrap Jesus. "Moses said that she should be stoned; what do you say?" they asked. If He said, "Let the law take its course," He would have lost much of His following—men and women who had been sinners and outcasts but won by His mercy. If He forgave He would defy the Jewish law. But He replied, "Let him that is without sin among you cast the first stone," then stopped, so that His eyes might not be upon them, and wrote in the sand. When He looked up, He and the woman were alone. "Does no man condemn thee?" He asked. "No man, Lord," the truly repentant woman replied. "Neither do I condemn thee," He answered, but linked with that forgiving word the stern injunction, "Go and sin no more!"

Repentance, a sincere turning away from the evil; forgiveness, a spirited effort for a better life supported by the very power of God—here is the sovereign cure for the sense of guilt. God's cure. And with such assurance of forgiveness, and the imparting of a new power for daily living, will come an inner sense of peace which promotes our total well-being. We may be very sure that, as Frederick Faber sang:

> There's a wideness in God's mercy
> Like the wideness of the sea;
> There's a kindness in His justice,
> Which is more than liberty. . . .
>
> For the love of God is broader
> Than the measure of man's mind;
> And the heart of the Eternal
> Is most wonderfully kind.

CHAPTER 15

Where Religion Goes Beyond Reason

FOR NEARLY A quarter of a century I was a teacher in a theological seminary. Most of our students preached occasionally and some of them regularly as part-time pastors of churches. One of the constant dangers in which our students stood as preachers was that of carrying their class-room attitudes and problems into the pulpit. In school we were inevitably, and quite properly, concerned with a variety of problems related to religion—questions as to the validity of the religious ideology transmitted to us by our culture, or as to the possibility of any rational basis for religious faith, and much else. But religious experience cannot be regarded as identical with its theological formulation. Religion is not theorizing about religion. It is not a set of dogmas, however correct. Religion is a phase of life, an attitude toward life, a way of living; indeed, it may be said to be life itself, life at its best. Religion lies deep-rooted in human needs, aspirations, desires. In religion man seeks a consciously adequate life; he seeks to effect a satisfying adjustment of himself as a person to the totality of his environment; he seeks a sense of completeness and fulfilment, of utter and satisfying self-realization in a community which supports and sustains him. He seeks life, and life more abundantly.

The danger in which our students stood, then, was that of carrying into the pulpit the intellectual problems with which they were wrestling and thus failing in their primary obligation of leading their people into that fulness of life which is the essence of Christian religious experience. The function of the Christian preacher is to lead his people "to know (not merely as an intellectual concept, but as a vital experience) the love of Christ which passeth knowledge (as intellectually conceivable), that they might be filled with all the fulness of God."

Religion, then, is something more than any theory of the universe, or any idea about God, or any intellectual formulation whatsoever. It is the quest itself, the search and the drive for values and for an experience, which gives lasting satisfaction. An experience of religion cannot be fully explained by setting forth the ideas which are involved in it, nor even by a logical or psychological analysis of that experience. It is so with any vital human experience. Take the experience of home. A home may be analyzed and described in terms of its construction, the persons who live together in it, the relationships these persons sustain to one another, the activities they pursue; even the values which the members discover in living together may be set forth. But in the actuality of experience, is this home? Home is something which you know in more profound and intangible ways than as an intellectual concept.

One may know the love of home in a way that passes knowledge:

> Strength of a man, a woman's song, laugh of a child,
> Though dark the night without, and wild
> The storm o'erhead!
> O little homes, set forth on every hand,
> Ye little walled-in worlds of joys and fears,
> Built on the common place of smiles and tears,
> Ye are the strength and sinew of the land.

And religion, like home, is indeed something more than an intellectually respectable organization of ideas about it. Religion is the quest of humanity for life in its wholeness and richness, the search of mankind for complete and satisfying adjustment and fulfilment.

Now the practical significance of this ought to be that we recognize clearly that, however important it is that we think clearly about religion—and that is very important, we can scarcely spend too much effort in the endeavor—it is still more important that we experience a rich and satisfying religious life. One may think very clearly and correctly and have a very barren religious experience while, on the other hand, one may entertain the most fantastic theological concepts and yet enjoy a rewarding and sustaining religious experience. Of course it is the task of the intellect to keep religion sane, and to keep it from taking superstitious and irrational forms, indeed, to lead it into the most fruitful and effective expressions. But it is easily possible by too exclusive emphasis upon the intellectual aspects of religion to destroy even more fundamental values.

Some years ago I heard the late beloved Professor J. M. P. Smith, of the University of Chicago (who certainly required of his own students severe intellectual discipline), tell a group of Divinity students about a girl whom he knew who had recently returned home after four years spent in an Eastern college. Her aesthetic tastes had been cultivated to a point where everything at home seemed crude and unbearable. The furniture was ugly, the pictures atrocious, and the rugs simply could not be endured. And so she started in ruthlessly to set things right without any regard for the fact that her parents' affections were deeply attached to these familiar things which had somehow become bound up with all the joys and sorrows they had shared through the years. For them, the aesthetic improvement of their home left it a much less lovely place, and the harshness with which the change was effected constituted a near tragedy. Professor Smith compared that performance with that of many a theological student or emancipated young minister, who ruthlessly tears out the cherished convictions of people in his congregation without any regard for other values which are torn out and thrown on the scrap-heap with the intellectual rubbish.

I am not arguing for obscurantism in religion. I am only pointing out that other values besides the intellectual are involved, and that they must be carefully conserved while we are trying to set our ideas right. First things should come first. And, unfortunately, incalculable damage has sometimes been done by failure to recognize priority of religious experience over its supporting intellectual structure.

Baron von Hügel, the Roman Catholic thinker who used to find some of his most stimulating intellectual companions among Protestants, tells a story which illustrates this primacy of religious experience over intellectual formulations. He once told of a young American skeptic who confessed to Dr. James Martineau that he had become skeptical of his own religious doubt, and asked Dr. Martineau if he could give him any assistance in thinking through his problem. Dr. Martineau advised him to try an experiment. He advised him to live for a few months with believing people, then move for another equal period of time and live in a community of unbelievers. The young skeptic went to Germany, and for six months lived among devout Westphalian peasants. He found them crude, slow-minded, and even superstitious, but they did know how to meet the great crises of life—birth, death, bereavement, love, suffering and sin. They sustained a relationship with unseen forces which gave them serenity and strength for daily living. Then, for six months, he lived among university students in Berlin. They were brilliant, witty, informed, and delightful companions, but before the great crises of life they were helpless. They possessed no inner resources, they had no sustaining faith.

This does not mean that clear thinking about religion is of no consequence. We need as clear concepts as we can frame of God and of his relationship with His world and with man. We need the best possible intellectual tools. It is particularly important in dealing with children and young people that we should not present Christianity in an intellectual framework which will later have to be discarded because that framework is seen to be untenable in the light of scientific facts. St. Thomas Aquinas was quite right in his insistence that dogma must not be contrary to reason. But primacy belongs to the experience rather than to its intellectual formulation.

The fact is that we need both genuine experience of religion and clear thinking about it. F. W. Robertson of Brighton, the great British preacher of a past generation, tells of the dark hour through which he passed when he came to see that many of the intellectual premises upon which he had built his faith were false.

It is an awful moment [he said], when the soul begins to find that the props on which it has blindly rested so long, are, many of them, rotten, and begins to suspect them all; when it begins to doubt if there is anything to believe at all. It is an awful hour—let him who has passed through it say how awful—when this life has lost its meaning, and seems shrivelled into a span; when the grave appears to be the end of all, human goodness nothing but a name, and the sky above this universe a dead expanse, black with the void from which God Himself has disappeared. . . . I know but one way in which a man may come forth from his agony scatheless; it is by holding fast to those things which are certain still—the grand, simple landmarks of morality. . . . If there be no God and no future state, yet even then it is better to be generous than selfish, better to be chaste than licentious, better to be true than false, better to be brave than a coward. Blessed is the man who, in the tempestuous darkness of the soul, has dared to hold fast to these venerable landmarks. . . . Thrice blessed, because his night shall pass into clear bright day.

The remedy, when an examination of the evidence shows that the intellectual assumptions upon which we have reared our structure of religious faith are false, is not to close our eyes and assert the more strongly that they are true. That is the way of bigotry, the defence of the frightened. The way out is not by refusing to think and to trust one's mind, but to think more deeply, to examine the evidence more carefully, to commit oneself to following the truth wherever it may lead, being assured that God is truth. "Ye shall know the truth," said Jesus, "and the truth shall make you free." So it was with Robertson. He affirmed the truth that he knew, and God led him into more truth, until he came out of the darkness of doubt into the bright day of an enlightened faith, and became England's greatest preacher of the liberating Gospel of Christ.

Religion needs both vital experience and clear thinking about it. If religion lacks vitality and immediacy it is powerless; if it is supported by ideas which are false, it will deteriorate into superstition, or it may be lost altogether. But there is, fortunately, no conflict between genuine religion and sound thinking. A vital Christian experience, supported by a sound structure of thought will stand secure without danger of lapse into either fanaticism, superstition or sentimentalism.

But religion, without becoming irrational, goes beyond reason. We may know the love of Christ which passeth knowledge. To know that love and be filled with God's fulness is to experience Christian life in a profounder sense than can be set forth in any statement about it. So to know God's love is to enter into an experience of rich and satisfying living; it is to find oneself sustained by Powers far beyond human comprehension; it is to achieve a sense of being "at one with the Universe," happily related to one's neighbors and to one's God. This is, indeed, "the abundant life."

In what sense, then, may religion go beyond reason without becoming contrary to reason?

In exactly the same way that love goes beyond reason without being contrary to reason. Love, friendship and religion represent different orders of experience from intellectual analysis and the organization of structures of ideas. The former belong in the area of personal response and relationship; the latter in the area of manipulation and control.

Professor George M. Mead, in his classes on social psychology, used to make a sharp distinction between the social and mechanical attitudes. The *mechanical* attitude is that impersonal attitude which we take toward things, for purposes of manipulation and control, although, indeed, one may take a mechanical attitude toward persons, as when an industrialist thinks of his employees as "hands," mere parts of the machinery of production. The social attitude, on the other hand, is that which we take toward persons, as persons, when, for example, we feel the warm handclasp of a friend. It is not manipulation and control we seek here, but personal response. It is true that we constantly slip from one attitude into another. I recall stepping into a hospital elevator once, and saying to the operator, "Third floor, please." The operator was, for my present purposes, only part of the mechanism. But the operator replied, "Well, don't you recognize your friends?" And immediately the emotional quality of the experience changed, for the operator was my boy's chum, as well as the son of one of my own closest personal friends. The personal rather than the mechanical attitude immediately became dominant as we inquired about each other's families.

Now, religion is precisely the adoption of that social attitude toward those cosmic forces upon which man is dependent and which we name God. It is quite true that we often take the mechanical attitude toward cosmic forces. That is precisely what the scientist does, in order that he may understand their modes of working and thus manipulate and control them. The scientific fallacy is to suppose that this is the only appropriate attitude to take toward these mysterious powers. Religion adopts toward these forces personal attitudes, and seeks fellowship and response. And men, through all the ages, have felt that, in seeking to establish such a relationship, they have not been disappointed. If one asks why men take this attitude toward the ultimate cosmic forces upon which life depends, the only answer seems to be that that is the way in which man is constituted. He is made for fellowship, not only with his fellow-man, but with his God. Faith ventures the conviction, which certainly goes beyond reason but is not contrary to reason, that the adoption of a personal attitude toward the Source and Support of our lives is justified; that that Reality "in which we live and move and have our being," whatever more it may be (for in all its fulness it "passes knowledge"), is a Will and Purpose with which we may have fellowship and cooperate, and that to enter into such a relationship is to find life's deepest meaning and fulfilment. God is "center and soul of every sphere, yet to each loving heart how near." St. Augustine expressed the profoundest aspiration of man, when he said: "O God, Thou madest us for Thyself, and our hearts are restless until they find rest in Thee." And the Psalmist cried, "As panteth the hart after the waterbrooks, so longeth my soul after Thee, O God!"

True religion is, then, the experience of that "abundant life" which Jesus said He had come to bestow. It is a life adequately adjusted to the rich and ever enlarging opportunities of human experience. What lifts man above the brute is the vast potentialities which he possesses for wider experience. Unnumbered aspirations, capacities and ideals are the treasures of men of which the lower orders of creation know nothing; to be awakened, responsive, released, adjusted to all this, is to enter into life.

Few men, unfortunately, live as fully as they might. I recall once, while a student in Toronto, going to hear Paderewski play in Massey Hall. My seat was a cheap one in the topmost gallery, but the superb music of that master pianist reached us clear and full as it wafted up to our lofty perch. My attention was attracted to a young couple seated a few rows in front of me. The girl was absolutely fascinated, reaching far forward so as not to miss the faintest note. But the young man sat back in his seat. Every now and again he would look around at the listening audience, then at the fascinated girl, then curiously down at the stage where Paderewski sat at the piano. Then he would slowly shake his head. His whole demeanor seemed to say, "There really must be something in it, or so many people would not be interested. But it is certainly not for me."

The response of many people toward many aspects of life is very similar to that. They are not aware and responsive. By just so much their lives are poorer than they might be. The abundant life is the one fully responsive to this vast, mysterious, and wonderful world in which our lives are set.

But the most important and inclusive of all these responses is that which we make, as persons, to that great Goodness who calls us to fellowship with Himself. To become aware that a Heart of Love encompasses us, that a good Will and Purpose directs us, that "the high and mighty One that inhabits eternity condescends to dwell with him that is of a humble and contrite spirit," is to enter into an experience that transcends all other possible life-enriching experiences. It is the knowing of a Love that passeth knowledge. It is being filled with all the fulness of God.

There is no better way into that experience than by the process which the old mystics used to describe as "the practice of the presence of God." To come with reverence and utter devotion into the presence of that Ultimate Reality in the midst of which our lives are set, there to dedicate ourselves to the loftiest purpose to which life may be given, is certainly one of the very best means available of achieving a dominant purpose which shall unify our wayward and discordant impulses, and bring to us a sense of happy adjustment which is at the heart of all true religious experience. Moreover, it is something which we must ourselves experience before we can share.

If God is, indeed, the living God, this is not only an experience that men enjoyed in some bygone time; it is an experience for men here and now. In his new book, *A Call to What is Vital*, Rufus Jones the great Quaker mystic of Haverford College, tells of his own experience back in 1886 during a solitary walk in the foothills of the Alps. He says:

I felt the walls grow thin between the visible and the invisible, and there came a sudden flash of eternity, breaking in on me. I kneeled down then and there in the forest glade, in sight of the mountains, and dedicated myself in the hush and silence, but in the presence of an invading life, to the work of interpreting the deeper nature of the soul, and direct mystical relation with God, which had already become my major interest.[1]

This is a knowledge of the reality and the love of God which goes beyond knowledge as scientifically ascertained and verified. But it has been the sustaining experience of multitudes. Out of such a living experience one may say that he *knows* God, not merely knows about Him. As Rufus Jones says in the same book:

Vital religion cannot be maintained and preserved on the

[1] From *A Call to What Is Vital*, p. 71, by Rufus M. Jones. Copyright 1948 by The Macmillan Company and used with their permission.

theory that God dealt with our human race only in the far past ages, and that the Bible is the only evidence we have that our God is *a living, revealing, communicating God.* If God ever spoke He is still speaking. He is *the Great I am,* not the Great He was . . ." [2]

When little, blind, deaf and dumb Helen Keller, under the marvellously patient and intelligent guidance of her teacher, Miss Sullivan, had learned to communicate with others, her parents felt that she should immediately have religious instruction. She was taken to Phillips Brooks, the great Boston preacher, and he told her as simply as he could about God. And Helen Keller replied, "I have always known that there was such a One, but I did not know His name." Unfortunately there are many seeing and hearing people whose eyes are more tightly closed, and whose ears are more firmly sealed, than those of the little blind and deaf girl. To have our eyes opened that we may see Him, our ears unsealed that we may hear His voice, will mean entrance into a more abundant life than we have ever hitherto known.

[2] *Ibid.,* p. 65.